GATHER IN MY NAME

SILVESTER O'FLYNN OFM Cap

Gather in My Name

GOSPEL MEDITATIONS FOR PRAYER GROUPS,
HOLY HOURS OR PERSONAL PRAYER

THE COLUMBA PRESS
1993

First edition, 1993, published by
THE COLUMBA PRESS
93 The Rise, Mount Merrion, Blackrock, Co Dublin, Ireland

Cover and illustrations by Bill Bolger
Origination by The Columba Press
Printed in Ireland by
Colour Books Ltd, Dublin

ISBN 185607 070 0

Nihil Obstat:
Patrick Muldoon DD
Censor Deputatus

Imprimatur:
✠ Séamus Hegarty
Bishop of Raphoe

Scripture quotations are taken from *Christian Community Bible*, published in the Philippines by Claretian Publications, St Paul Publications and Divine Word Publications.

Contents

Introduction

This book is offered to all who would like to meet together for prayer, but are looking for help to structure their meetings. Hopefully it will also appeal to individuals who seek guidance in meditating on the gospel.

It is inspired by the sacred word of God in the gospel, particularly by the experiences of those who met with Jesus in the ups and downs of life. Their meetings with Jesus can instruct us on how to conduct our meetings with the Lord.

I have a picture in my mind of people gathered in a circle around the open book of God's word. Each person is in a different expression of prayer, like separate planets around the central sun. I see one person with hands open in petition: another is beating breast in sorrow. One face is bright in joyful adoration, but another is tense and paining. This person is happy and celebrating while this other is shattered by bad news. We come to pray out of many different situations, moods, feelings and experiences. Just as people came to Jesus out of their various situations of life.

Each meeting in this book begins with a typical life-situation. We begin by reaching out to Jesus, seeking to touch even the hem of his garment, in our stumbling, stuttering words. The next step is to listen to a reading from the gospel and to ponder on it in silence. Group members might then share with the others what the gospel means to them. This is called reflecting on the word. I have offered some ideas towards understanding the text and applying it to life.

The next stage of the meeting is a listening prayer. Jesus speaks to us in reply to our prayer. We listen in our heart. He tells us of his constant love, his personal care and his sure support in our lives. He is the Good Shepherd whose word guides us along the right path towards those restful waters where we drink of the Holy Spirit who dwells within us.

I have not given any particular opening or closing prayers for each meeting. I think it preferable to let each little community pray in whatever way they are most comfortable. Some will pray in a traditional formula, some will express their prayer in song and another group will be happy to compose informal prayers as the occasion demands.

It will be helpful if each meeting has a leader, not necessarily the host for the night. The leader guides the meeting along from stage to stage, asks people to do the various readings, introduces the times of silent reflection and gently invites group reflection. Obviously, the leader must have prepared beforehand.

'Where two or three are gathered in my name, I am there with them.' (Mt 18:20)

The Leader

– prepares beforehand and is familiar with the text for each meeting:

– invites people to be quiet and to pray for the help of the Holy Spirit:

– guides the meeting along from stage to stage:

– asks people to read the various parts:

– introduces the times of personal reflection and gently invites people to share their thoughts if they wish.

All Members of the Group

– use this book simply as the starting point for your own thoughts:

– put the book aside if it is restricting your own prayers:

– don't be afraid to share your own reflections:

– please don't let your meeting be only a reading session.

For a Holy Hour

– allow periods of silence or reflective music between the readings.

Joining a Group

Invite everybody to be quiet for about two minutes. Then let somebody lead the group in a prayer to the Holy Spirit. If a hymn is sung, so much the better.

You have been asked to come to a group who wish to meet regularly to pray together, to support one another's faith and to grow in their knowledge of Jesus Christ. For this first meeting as a group, we focus attention on how we are feeling about praying with others, our positive hopes for the group as well as our fears and apprehensions. So let us begin with a fairly typical person expressing his/her hopes and fears to Jesus.

Introductory Prayer

O Lord, I'm not sure what to think about this group prayer. Part of me thinks it is a very good idea to belong to a group. It should be a good discipline for me having a definite appointment with others on a set evening. I know all too well that I have made many resolutions about giving more time to prayer, but the plans never seem to get off the drawing board. Here is something definite, if I can make the commitment now to come to the group every week. It will test the sincerity of my resolution.

I have often enough tried on my own to spend a longish period at prayer but I usually give it up. Mainly because I wasn't getting much out of it. I hope that the support of other people will help me to get a much better understanding of prayer. Being lost on your own in a fog of doubt is a lonely business. So, I'll take a chance on joining the group.

However, Lord, I have to admit that I am very apprehensive

about a few areas. I am not accustomed to all this business of sharing. It threatens me. I was brought up in the old style, where one's inner religion was a very private affair. It was very personal, just between God and yourself. If prayer went well you didn't boast about it. And if it did not go well, you kept it to yourself. Even when we said the family rosary, we turned our backs on one another and faced into our own chairs or private corners. So, the idea of sharing with others is new to me.

Another fear that I have, Lord, is that I will have nothing to offer. I can see myself being ashamed if I have little or nothing to contribute. And on the other hand I dread the prospect of somebody who will totally take over a meeting and dominate everybody. No fault of their own perhaps, for it might be a sort of nervous energy that feels the need to fill up every moment of silence.

There will probably be evenings when I will find it very hard to face the group. But these occasions when I am feeling down will probably be the very times that I most need the support of the group. When I least feel like coming will be when I most need to come.

So, these are my fears, Lord. I know that you always told people 'Be not afraid.' This time I'll try to take you at your word. Good Shepherd, lead me. Let me hear your voice calling in the sacred word of scripture. Help me to leave the confines of an isolated religion to know all the support that a group gathered in your name can offer.

 *Take some minutes in silent reflection on your hopes from the group and on your fears and apprehensions. Then any person who wishes may share their reflections with the others.*

A reading from the holy gospel according to Matthew (18:19-20)

I say to you: If on earth two of you are united in asking for anything, it will be granted to you by my heavenly Father. For where two or three are gathered in my name, I am there with them.

Spend some time thinking about this gospel passage, picking up the words or phrases or images that appeal to you. You might wish to exchange ideas with the other people in your group.

Reflecting on the word

This passage is taken from Matthew's gospel. One of the key ideas of Matthew is that Jesus means that God is with us. At the beginning of his gospel, Matthew refers to Jesus as Emmanuel, which means God-is-with-us. And at the closing of the gospel, Matthew quotes the promise of the risen Lord to be with his disciples until the end of time.

In the passage under consideration, Jesus is speaking of life in the community of the church. The emphasis is on the community nature of the church. Christianity is not a religion for an isolated spirituality.

Many of us have inherited a very self-centred idea of salvation and a very private idea of prayer. Ever since the move away from a central teaching authority to the private interpretation of the bible, there has been a strong tendency towards an individualistic spirituality. People have put great emphasis on the need to save-my-soul, while overlooking their social obligations.

When Jesus spoke of salvation he did not confine his meaning to getting into heaven in the next life. Salvation, in the mind of Jesus, is also concerned with improving the quality of life for people in this world too. That is why our missionaries bring more than the written bible to people. They must also proclaim God's love in setting up educational facilities, health programmes and human development schemes. Charity is the essence of Christian spirituality. So, holy talk is but an empty shell unless it is backed up by practical action. And a prayerlife that never shares with others is incomplete.

Jesus solemnly promised to be with the community of his church. There is no such thing as a one-person church. But wherever a group of people gather in Christ's name, there is the beginning of church. Take Jesus at his word that he has promised to be with the community, even of two or three, who gather in his name.

Let us pray
O Lord, may we strongly believe that you are with us as we gather in your name. Lord, hear us.
As we come together in a little community, may we accept our differences and enrich one another in faith. Lord, hear us.
Broaden our view of salvation and make us less self-centred in prayer. Lord, hear us.

Invite people to add any prayers they wish. Then allow a time of silence to listen to the Lord in one's heart.

Jesus replies

My dear friend, I welcome you as you venture out of your private little house to share with others. I promise to be with you in your group. As you find me in other people, to the same extent you will become aware of my presence in you. A gathering of people becomes a little church community when you all begin to recognise that it is my presence which is the common bond between you. The Holy Spirit will teach you in a wisdom that will grow in your hearts.

Do not be afraid to come out of your private little shell. There is no need to feel ashamed that you have no gems of intelligence to offer. It is okay to be needy. How can I ever give you anything unless you are aware of your poverty: unless you come to me with empty hands.

Come to me with humility. Then I can do something for you. I fill the hungry with good things but the proudhearted go empty away.

Come to me with faith: enough faith to set you in a positive frame of mind. Come with an Easter faith. Believe that I am risen and that I am with my church until the end of time. Believe that I shall be with the community who gather in my name.

I am your priest who intercedes for you with the Father. I am the head of the body of which you are together the members. I am the vine and my Spirit flows through you, my branches. And it is the one Spirit who gives life to you and to the other members. You must get beyond yourself, to grow in awareness of all that you share with the others.

Come with charity in your heart. Do not look on personal differences as a threat but see them as enriching the group. Let there be a loving acceptance of one another in the gathering so that a sense of deep security will develop. Regard each individual with deep respect as somebody whom I love. And treat everything that is said with the utmost confidentiality. Only in this secure friendship can one's inner life blossom and grow. I promise that you will be amazed when you see people growing in confidence and self-esteem before your very eyes. Miracles still happen when I am present.

My dear friend, do not be afraid to come out of the narrow cell of your self-centred prayer. Open up your doors so that others can come in to your spiritual life and that you might go out to them. In finding the depths of other people you will be finding me in a new way.

Close the meeting with a hymn or prayer of thanksgiving.

Praying with Scripture

Let everybody be quiet for about two minutes. Then ask the Holy Spirit to inspire your group in heart and in mind.

 In this meeting with Jesus we face up to the fact that very few of us are accustomed to using the bible for prayer. It may be a new experience using the gospel as the source of our thoughts and words.

Introductory Prayer

O Lord, I have taken my courage in hand to come along to pray with other people. It's not easy, Lord. Yet I feel happy that I have come so far. Relieved that I have broken a barrier. I hope that with the others supporting me, we will all learn how to pray better.

But I must admit that I am still very apprehensive. I suppose I am a creature of the old ways and somewhat afraid of new demands. The fear of coming out into the open with my personal beliefs would finish me altogether.

I feel quite anxious about what we will do at each meeting. Where will we get our ideas from? Will we be sharing shallow experiences or endlessly repeating ourselves in an effort to keep things going?

I hear we will be using portions of the gospel at each meeting. I am familiar with the general outline of the gospel stories as I hear them often enough at Mass. But it will be a new experience using the gospel as a source of personal prayer. I am excited at the prospect of learning a lot about prayer from your own words, Lord.

I do hope, Lord, that we will be safe with the bible. I know that sounds strange. But there are people today who quote the bible morning, noon and night but they do not believe in going to Mass nor in praying to your Blessed Mother. So, Lord, may our group be inspired in the truth and not go off the rails from sound doctrine.

So, I have a certain hesitation about a group like us delving into the bible on our own. It is like watching your mother baking a cake but the first time you do it on your own is a bit nervewracking. Or learning how to drive with the instructor beside you is okay until you venture out into the traffic on your own for the first time.

We are banking on your help, Lord, to guide us safely through our meetings. Teach us how to read your gospel as a source of true faith and as an inspiration to prayer.

 *You might wish to chat among yourselves for a little while about your use of the bible. Do you ever read it privately? Is it part of your regular prayer? How could it be dangerous?*

A reading from the holy gospel according to Luke (8:11-15)

Now this is the point of the parable of the sower. The seed is the word of God. Those along the wayside are people who hear it, but immediately the devil comes and takes the word from their minds, for he doesn't want them to believe and be saved. Those on the rocky ground are those who receive the word with joy, but they have no root; they believe for a while but give way in time of temptation. Among the thorns are people who hear the word but as they go their way, are choked by worries, riches and the pleasures of life; they bring no fruit to maturity. The good soil, instead, are people who received the word and keep it in a gentle and generous mind, and persevering patiently, they bear fruit.

Chat for a while on your own ideas from this gospel reading. Has God's word been a seed in your life ... growing and bearing fruit?

Reflecting on the Word

Jesus has given his sacred word to us as a seed destined to grow. Our prayer will be of very low quality unless we draw light from the inspired word of the bible. St Jerome, a great scholar of the bible, maintained that ignorance of the bible is ignorance of Christ. How can we sustain a relationship with Jesus unless we listen to his words?

The word of God is a seed and our heart is the ground that receives the seed. But it all depends on what kind of soil we have to offer.

We can be like that soil by the wayside, never opened by the plough. Sunday after Sunday we hear the word but little or nothing sinks in. By Monday morning would we remember yesterday's gospel? Far too many Catholics are wayside soil, never paying the slightest attention to God's word.

Then there's the rocky ground. That stands for superficial piety which has no deep roots. Superficial piety is okay so long as we are getting nice religious experiences at prayer. But if we are not feeling turned on, or getting clear answers, then we do not last too long. This sort of shallow piety is not enough.

The third soil is good but, unfortunately, too many briars and weeds have been let grow unchecked. Anybody who wants a genuine prayerlife must lead a disciplined life. Every gardener has to keep the weeds in check. The briars which choke prayer are anxious fretting about the future, too much interest in material possessions and the uncontrolled pursuit of pleasure.

In good soil where the weeds are controlled, we can look forward to a life growing richly with the word of God. Notice the lovely qualities of people who let God's word be the source of their growth. They are gentle; they have a generous mind; and they persevere in patience.

Gentle with oneself, not too anxious and not demanding perfect results.

Generous with others, in mind, in word and in action.

Persevering with God even when his ways are beyond our understanding.

Let us pray

O Lord, we desire to be receptive soil to your word as we read it, discuss it and prayerfully ponder on it. Lord, hear us.

Lord, through the wisdom of your word may we grow in gentleness of heart, generosity of mind and patience of soul. Lord, hear us.

O Lord, help us to overcome our fear of sharing with one another. Lord, hear us.

Encourage people to add their own ideas and prayers.

Jesus replies

My beloved friend, it makes me very happy that you now desire to learn more about prayer and especially about my word to you in the bible. My word will be a lamp for your steps and a light for your mind.

I know you have a passing acquaintance with the gospel. But this is only secondhand experience. You only listen to it through the voice of some other person. You are missing the excitement of a firsthand, personal meeting. Surely you are not afraid of meeting me and listening to my words!

Come and meet me in a personal encounter. Remember, I love you. And I have many important words to whisper to you in the quietness of your heart. Words from my heart for you alone.

It makes me sad that while I love people so much, yet few take my personal love seriously. I have so much that I want to say to the depths of their souls but few come to listen. Many come to talk to me but they do not bother to listen. No wonder you were fitted out with two ears and only one mouth, for your Creator-Father knew you would find it twice as hard to listen as to speak! Sadly, the holy bible is far too often a sort of house ornament which looks good on the shelf but is never taken to read.

Up to this, your prayerlife has been on a starvation diet. You have condemned yourself to spiritual anorexia by your failure to eat at the table of my word.

For too long you have made the mistake of thinking that only the few were called to something more than saying prayers. And for too long you have left the scriptures to the specialists. Do you think that the everyday parables that I spoke were for specialists only! Or that my words were addressed to scholars alone.

So, my dear friend, let go of all your fears about taking up the bible. Come to me to sit at my feet as you ponder on my word.

Come with humility as you recognise your need for divine guidance. I am the light of the world and without my word you will stray in darkness.

Come with earnest desire, thirsting for prayer, hungering for the rich food which will make you grow.

Come in an attitude of faith and prayer, and always ask the help of the Holy Spirit to make my words come alive in you.

Come in an Easter faith, expecting to meet me on the road with words for your life. Remember the disciples who met me on the road to Emmaus. How their hearts took fire as they listened to my word! Come and walk the road of life with me, eager to receive my word for your souls's delight.

Close the meeting with an appropriate hymn or prayer

With Open Doors

First come to silence to prepare for prayer. Then ask the help of the Holy Spirit for your group.

When we come to pray we must try to let our lives be totally open to Jesus. We must try to set aside our obsessive thoughts and to calm down our compulsive drives so as to sit down and be attentive to God alone. We are forced to admit that sometimes the Lord may be knocking at our door but our rooms are locked.

Introductory Prayer

Dear Lord, I come to spend some time with you in prayer. I really must do something to improve my prayer-life. It's an area that always leaves me feeling guilty. I'm never comfortable with it, I never seem to be satisfied. I am always making resolutions to pray better. I have made more resolutions about prayer than about any other area of life.

I secretly envy those who are comfortable with their prayer. I envy the way they seem to be absorbed in thought, totally at ease and quiet in themselves. My problems start when I cannot relax. I don't find much restfulness in prayer. My mind never stays put but is always hopping about after every possible distracting thought.

My heart does not slow down when I try to relax. Instead, pressure comes on to be up and at it. There is always something I remember that must be done. I am one of those people who are better at giving than receiving. Ask me to do something for you, Lord, and generally I have no problem. But having to sit quietly and wait to receive is not my strong suit.

I sense a deep need to stop all this running about. I suspect that I should minister more to my own needs occasionally. I often find myself wishing I might meet someone with whom I can really open up. Though I'm not quite sure what exactly I want to open out. But I feel there are doors which have been closed on parts of my life. And I have even forgotten what is closed off. I'm almost afraid at this stage of what might be in there. Maybe there's nothing to be afraid of.

Needless to say, Lord, distractions are an ongoing problem. Prayer, for me, usually equals a battle with distractions. And if that is not bad enough, when the distractions are about people the thoughts are rarely complimentary. They are usually very negative, very sore thoughts. Usually blaming people.

Now I wonder whether all these people of my thoughts are the problem or am I the problem. Am I projecting my own discontent onto others? I will use anything or anybody to cover up what I ought to face in myself.

You know, Lord, it's a long time since I was so honest about myself.

As you can see I am very mixed up about my prayer. I do want to pray. I deeply desire your Holy Spirit. Teach me to pray, just as you taught your disciples to pray.

Fill me with the power of the Holy Spirit to inspire my prayer. Open up your sacred word to me that I might receive your light upon my life. Without you I can do nothing. But with you all things are possible. For you are the way, the truth and the life.

 *Reflect in silence on your problems in relaxing in prayer. After a little while people may share their experiences.*

A reading from the holy gospel according to Luke (10:38-42)

As Jesus and his disciples were on their way, he entered a village and a woman called Martha welcomed him to her house. She had a sister named Mary who sat down at the Lord's feet to listen to his words. Martha, meanwhile, was busy with all the serving and finally she said, 'Lord, don't you care that my sister has left me to do all the serving?'

But the Lord answered, 'Martha, Martha, you worry and are troubled about many things, whereas only one thing is needed. Mary has chosen the better part, and it will not be taken away from her.'

Before reading any further share your own feelings about this incident.

Reflecting on the Word

Martha met Jesus with a welcome. But it was not a total welcome. Certainly her house and table were open to him but there were many rooms in her life which were closed off from inspection.

She was distracted with all the serving. The door of her attention was closed. Serving what? Nice little extras to the meal. It made her feel good. But was she serving the Lord's needs or her own need to feel indispensable? How could the house ever get on without her? It had become an obsession with her, leaving her no time for sitting and no space for listening.

Martha spoke to Jesus, not just as friend to friend, but with deep reverence. She called him 'Lord'. But then she went on to make a double complaint: that the Lord did not care and that her sister would not help. A complaining prayer is all about the all important ME. 'Please tell her, Lord, to help me.'

There we go again, our favourite prayer. 'Lord, my will be

done. Please change other people and their ways so that my will might be done.' Talk about doors being closed to Jesus! And all the while we fancy that we have welcomed him into our house.

Martha implied that her sister was the problem. But Jesus showed that it was she who was agitated and fretful. He asked her to accept responsibility for her reactions and to own her emotions. 'You worry and fret about so many things,' not only about Mary but about many things.

We link the scene with our own inner behaviour. Pay attention to any areas of life that have been touched by the story. Are there any embers of memory that have been fanned back into flame?

Have we ever gone so far as to complain, like Martha, that the Lord no longer cares for us? That our prayers have not been heard? I'm sure that we have all prayed about the problems that other people have caused for us. Life would be grand only for so-'n-so. It's my sister is the problem, Lord, my father, my son, my neighbour...!

Perhaps we'd be surprised to have it pointed out to us that the agitation and fretting is our own. Granted, the other person may be wrong, but the negative reaction is mine.

If I cannot any longer relax with people at home,
if I cannot stay sitting for a full meal,
if I cannot listen to others and enjoy a conversation,
if my first thought about somebody here is a complaint ...
then I have become a problem to myself. And probably a problem to others too. There are many doors that I have closed off from myself, from others and from God.

Let us pray.
Lord, help us to be still and know that you are God. Lord, hear us.
O Jesus, may we have the wisdom to know what you called the better part of life. Lord, hear us.

Lord, help us to discern when you want us to work like Martha and when we are to be still like Mary. Lord, hear us.

Please add your own prayers or reflection

Jesus replies

My dear friend, I am so happy to visit you. I am happy to find you at home, coming in from the street of noise and activity as you make time for prayer.

You have invited me to come into your house. Thank you, dear friend. You know that I have chosen you and blessed you with the gift of faith. You have been blessed also in the good friends who support your faith.

Sometimes, though, I question the sincerity of your invitation. You talk to me at the front door as if you were ashamed to let me see the mess behind you. Do you think that I do not know it already? That you can hide things from me?

And there are days when you just talk at me! You never stop to listen. You talk at me in a torrent of words, white hailstones out of a black cloud. Words pounding at me. You are so wound up that you cannot listen.

And there are times when everything about you tells me that while you appear to welcome me, you'd much prefer if I hadn't called. Your mind is not available to me. Your attention is given elsewhere. You are not comfortable with me. I want to give you words of strength and peace but you won't let them in. Your inner doors are firmly bolted.

Look at how my friend, Mary of Bethany, received me. She simply sat at my feet and listened to me. Her welcome was total. She gave me her time and attention. The food she hungered for was my word. No obsession or compulsion could take it away from her. She stayed and listened and savoured my word, careful not to lose the least crumb.

My beloved friend, I cannot come to you unless you open

up your doors from the inside. You will not pray until you firmly decide to prefer your time with me to all your agitations and frettings.

'Look, I am standing at the door knocking. If one of you hears me calling and opens the door, I will come in to share his meal, side by side with him.' (Rev. 3:20)

Close the meeting with a suitable hymn or prayer.

Healing the Sources

Invite the group to be quiet and relax. Close your eyes for a few minutes'and invite Jesus to meet you here this evening. Somebody may then lead a prayer to the Holy Spirit.

 Our personal experiences have helped us to grow and develop our talents. But we are also the prisoners of our past, wounded by hurtful experiences, failures and misunderstandings. Our fears and anxieties, our obsessions and compulsions, our prejudices and blind spots all flow like a haemorrhage from deepseated sources in our past. This evening we invite Jesus to reach deeply into our hidden memory and heal us at the sources.

Introductory Prayer

O Jesus, I bring my whole life to you and invite you to touch every single moment of it with your warm, healing touch. You read me like an open book. You search me and you know me. You know me better than I know myself. There are places where the pages of my lifestory are stuck together and I can't get at them without damaging the story. There are pages where the ink of memory is too faded to read. And pages where the writing is so blotched that no human power can make sense of it.

But I can trust in you, Lord. I ask you to reach back into every hidden recess of memory, every corner of my heart. Wherever you find me wounded, paralysed, blinded or imprisoned, may your healing hand touch me, release me and heal me.

Let your love penetrate the darkness of my subconscious memories which I am unable to see. You know everything that has affected me from the first moment of my conception. Remove all barriers to wholeness which might have restricted me in the months while I was growing in my mother's womb. If there was any way in which my coming was not welcomed, now let your great love bridge the years and provide for what was absent.

If there were any physical or emotional trauma that I have carried since my emergence into this world, then, Lord, heal them in the soothing touch of your welcoming hand.

O Jesus of the gospel, you welcomed the little children and lovingly caressed them. Reach back into my childhood and heal me of any hurts I may be carrying from my earliest memories. If there was any lack of love, or attention, or care, that stunted my growth, now let your love hear my cries, soothe my soreness and strengthen me anew.

In my growing years, Lord, I could not escape being occasionally hurt by the faults of others: by their temper, their insensitivity, their jealousy, their drinking and the hundred guises of selfishness. Sometimes I was betrayed in confidences, let down by broken promises and misled by lies. In the sensitive years of adolescence I may have been hurt by teachers, by systems... even by your Church. Release me now from all the bitterness that remains and makes me paralysed and blinded in emotion.

If I have suffered through the sins and passions of others, help me to forgive them, Lord, with your forgiveness. Cleanse me totally of that sense of unworthiness that clings so forcibly to me. Free me from the deepseated obsessions and inhibitions which I have carried from my sexual awakening. Sanctify my sense of touch with the feeling of your love for all who reach out to me.

As you unroll the years, Lord, see those bruises left by any bitterness I had to endure. Heal the wounds of those encounters which left me frightened, which caused me to retreat unhealthily into my shell or erect barriers against people. Wherever I felt lonely, abandoned or rejected now grant me a new sense of worth as a person. Soothe and heal those wounds in my heart after the loss of a loved one through death or any other form of departure.

O Jesus, I now reach out to give and give over my life to you in total confidence. I invite you to manifest all that your sacred name means... Jesus... the one who saves his people. Save me from myself, Lord Jesus, save me from those parts of my life that have injured, blinded or imprisoned me.

I give you my entire self... my body, my mind, my imagination. And already I thank you for being JESUS ... Saviour ... Healer. I thank you for drawing me towards health, wholeness and freedom. Thank you, Lord Jesus, healer of body, mind and soul.

Stay awhile in silent reflection and bring your own bruised areas of life to Jesus. Then, if you wish, ask the others in the group to join you in prayer for some particular healing.

A reading from the holy gospel according to Mark (5:25-34)

Among the crowd was a woman who had suffered from bleeding for twelve years. She had suffered alot at the hands of many doctors and had spent everything she had, but instead of getting better, she was worse. Because she had heard about Jesus, this woman came up behind him and touched his cloak thinking, 'If I just touch his clothing, I shall get well.' Her flow of blood dried up at once, and she felt in her body that she was healed of her disease.

But Jesus was conscious that healing power had gone out from him, so he turned around in the crowd and asked, 'Who touched my clothes?' His disciples answered, 'You see how the people are crowding around you. Why do you ask who touched you?' But he kept looking around to see who had done it. Then the woman, aware of what had happened, came forward trembling and afraid. She knelt before him and told him the whole truth.

Then Jesus said to her, 'Daughter, your faith has saved you; go in peace and be free of this illness.'

GATHER IN MY NAME

Ponder in silence on the gospel story to pick up what was most significant for you. Then people might like to exchange their ideas.

Reflecting on the Word

Notice the phrase, 'the source of her bleeding dried up.' Long and painful treatment under various doctors had not touched the source of her problem. Having spent all she had with no marked improvement, it is understandable that her frustration only made her worse. True healing must get back to the source.

Suppose you are getting frequent headaches. Do you simply get rid of the pain by regularly swallowing tablets? Or do you regard the pain as having a message about something deeper? The source may be as simple as insufficient fresh air, lack of physical exercise, an unbalanced diet, pressure of work or a strained relationship.

'She had heard about Jesus'... and faith begins in hearing. The news about Jesus grew in her mind and reached her heart. Then faith gave birth to total confidence. Confidence gave her the courage to press forward and reach out to touch even the hem of his garment.

There is touching and touching, just as there is praying and praying. There is the sort of touching that the disciples referred to, that unavoidable physical contact whenever crowds are pressing and pushing: but there is also that special touch that Jesus felt, the faith-filled touch which drew power out of him. Just so, there is routine, half-hearted prayer; but there is also that faith-filled reaching out to God in prayer which releases his divine power.

Jesus told the woman where her healing came from: from her own faith. 'Your faith has restored you to health'. If the source of her complaint lay deeply within her, so too her healing had to come from within. Healing the sources usually requires us to get out of the prison of the prevailing situation. It may be a holy place, a gifted person, a sacred ritual, or the freedom to accept our story, which will be the medium of healing. When this woman touched the garment of Jesus she touched into such deep faith and confidence that she transcended the inner source of her troubles. And her faith brought her healing.

Let us pray.

Lord, give us that strong faith which will reach out and touch you in prayer. Lord, hear us.

Lord, lay your healing hands gently upon us. Lord, hear us.

Lord, help us to believe strongly in our contact with you in the sacraments of the church. Lord, hear us.

 *Invite people to express their own prayers.*

Jesus replies

My beloved one, I take you and accept you. I am so happy that you are now opening out your life to my healing power. My hands are locked until you find the key to release my power: and that key is your faith.

Take your life now to my church. I have given to my church the power to loose on earth whatever is loosed by my divine mercy in heaven. Take your lifestory to the beautiful sacrament of Reconciliation. It is there that you will meet me and reach out to touch me in your faith. I am not asking you to forget the past but to recall it and tell it to my priest who has been anointed in the power of the Holy Spirit to absolve you.

In telling your story you are humbly accepting your past as your own. But how few people properly appreciate this sacrament. It has become trivialized by a childish approach and a mechanical routine. It is part of the great story of my resurrection day, how my Father sent the Blessed Spirit to breathe the divine power of forgiveness upon the disciples. Come to me in this sacrament to receive my healing grace.

Come in your weakness to the table of the Eucharist. There you will find me every week, or every day if you wish, to be your food of life, your divine energy. When you meet me as your bread of life, what is there to fear ever again? Why be anxious when you know that you not only touch me but even eat and drink my energy unto yourself?

My dearly beloved one, your faith has brought you to this moment of peace and healing. Promise me now that you will not fall back into doubt again. Stay close to me in prayer. Accept the support of others who ask you to pray with them. Come to me regularly in the sacraments. My peace be with you now and always.

Close the meeting with a suitable prayer or hymn.

Do you want to let go ?

Relax in quietness for a few minutes. Think of Jesus and prepare to meet him. Invite somebody in the group to invoke the help of the Holy Spirit in your meeting.

 Sometimes when we come to meet Jesus we call out to him for help but he cannot give anything to us because our hands are not empty. We are holding on to some hurt memory or sinful desire which blocks his grace. We have to ask ourselves how sincere is our prayer.

Introductory Prayer

O Jesus, I come once more to you in prayer. But I am not at all comfortable. Something is upsetting me. I am worried about the sincerity of my prayers.

You see, Lord, I cry out to you and hold back from you at the same time. I ask you to help me overcome my sinfulness but I make little or no effort to change the way I carry on. I feel like St Augustine in the days when he prayed for purity but hoped it would not come for some while! I worry about the sincerity of my purpose of amendment.

We are complicated beings, aren't we, Lord. The way we pray for health in time of sickness but do nothing about a healthier lifestyle. The way we hold on to addictions which are harmful to our health.

Sometimes we even opt out of our responsibilities under the guise of prayer. We land our responsibilities into your lap. We will say prayers perhaps for those who have hurt us but take no practical steps to make it up with them. Or we pray for the hungry people of the world but never make any substantial sacrifice to help them. We're not totally honest about ourselves, are we, Lord.

My insincerity makes it hard for me to face you. It's okay to stay at a safe distance, anonymous in the crowd. It's easy enough to be carried along in church ceremonies. But coming face to face and looking at you eye to eye, speaking heart to heart, it's not easy, Lord.

You are all light and there is no hiding from you. You can read the heart. I carry a fear that you will see right through me and ask of me more than I am prepared to give. Maybe some day, Lord, I'll be ready to give all. But for the moment I am fearful. I am holding back. I am staying at a distance from you.

O Lord, give me courage. Courage to be very honest with myself and very sincere in all that I say to you. Help me to trust in you totally. To trust in you so that there is no holding back. When I hold out my hands to you, dear Lord, may they be fully open.

 *Reflect in silence on the areas of insincerity which hold you back from God. You may prefer to keep your thoughts to yourself but it is okay if people wish to share.*

A reading from the holy gospel according to John (5:1-9)

After this there was a feast of the Jews and Jesus went up to Jerusalem. Now, by the Sheep Gate in Jerusalem, there is a pool (called Bethzatha in Hebrew) surrounded by five galleries. In these galleries lay a multitude of sick people – blind, lame and paralysed – waiting for the water to move. For at times an angel of the Lord would descend into the pool and stir up the water; and the first person to enter after this movement of the water would be healed of whatever disease he had.

There was a man who had been sick for thirty-eight years. Jesus saw him, and since he knew how long this man had been lying there, he said to him, 'Do you want to be healed?' And the sick man answered, 'Sir, I have no one to put me into the pool when the water is disturbed; so while I am still on my way, another steps down before me.'

Jesus then said to him, 'Stand up, take up your mat and walk.' And at once the man was healed, and he took up his mat and walked.

Before reading further allow yourself time to draw out your own ideas from the passage. You may wish to share your ideas in the group.

Reflecting on the Reading

The episode seems to pivot around that surprising question of Jesus, 'Do you want to be healed?'

We are left to surmise what exactly happened at the pool. If we take what is said about the angel as literally true, then is strikes one that whatever healing took place was more like the lottery luck of being in the right place at the right time than a manifestation of divine compassion. If one is prepared to move beyond the literal sense of the words, the likely explanation is that periodically a fresh inflow, which was interpreted as the work of an angel, disturbed the water. And the belief had grown up that whoever was first in after that inflow would be cured. Whatever healing occured came from the patient's belief. Since a large percentage of bodily ailments are rooted in spiritual pain or internal stress, it stands to reason that the healing also must involve the inner world of imagination, memory and spirit. That is why Jesus had to challenge the man on the honesty of his wish to be well again.

It is recognised that sometimes people are partly in love with their illness or addiction or problem. This is called secondary gain. Getting well again might mean losing the attention of others, or letting go of the comforting blanket of self-pity. Or the return to health might mean having to take on responsibility for work, or home and family. The worst problem for some people would be having nothing to worry about!

It is interesting that the man did not answer the question as Jesus asked it. Instead he started dishing out blame. Blame on the vast anonymous group of A.N.Others who did not put poor me into the pool. Blame on those who got in before him. Jesus must have sensed this tendency to blame others rather than admit ownership of his condition. Hence his question which probed the sincerity of the man's heart.

The healing offered by Jesus was a combination of divine power and human cooperation. Once the man was willing to let go and to accept healing, then Jesus gave him a triple command: 'Stand up, take your mat and walk.' Perhaps the sleeping mat is an expression for the blanket of self-pity.

Further down in the chapter, when Jesus met him again he said to him: 'Now you are well; don't sin again, lest something worse happen to you.' (Jn 5:14) Jesus is warning him that if he returns to his negative, blaming mentality, his paralysis will come back in worse form. The former addict who returns to his drink or tobacco is quickly in deeper trouble than ever before.

We have to ask ourselves if the incident throws light on our own mental behaviour. Are we consoled at meeting Jesus? Or are we disturbed by his question, 'Do you want to let go?'

Let us pray.

Lord, save us from ourselves, especially from self-pity. Lord, hear us.

Lord, help us to trust you and to let go of all that restricts us. Lord, hear us.

Lord may we stop blaming others and accept responsibility for our own lives. Lord, hear us.

Allow people time for their own prayers.

Jesus replies

My poor friends, I love you. Do you really accept that? I'll say it to you again – I love you. I love you so much that I must challenge you to face the truth. Only the truth will set you free.

My challenge to you is – do you really want to be healed? Or do you want to hold on where you are because you cannot face the consequences? Have you some secret death-wish that makes you inflict harm on your wellbeing in body, mind and spirit?

I cannot cure you unless you positively desire life to the full. You must make the decision to get up and to embrace life and health. You must think positively about wanting to be fully alive in body, fully alert in mind and fully attentive in spirit. Embrace with love the life my Father has given you. Love your life enough to avoid anything that will harm or restrict it. Let go of any addiction that is harming your health.

You must pick up your sleeping mat, your comfort blanket, your self-pity wrapping. Please let go of your tendency to blame and whinge. Let go of those memories of where others hurt you or neglected you.

When a crisis blows up, remember that I am with you. Do not go back to your self-pity and martyr complex. There is nothing that the two of us, you and I together cannot overcome.

Walk into life with a fresh attitude. Let your mind be daily refreshed by the beautiful things of life. If the strident voices of radio or T.V., with their constant emphasis on bad news, upset you, then exercise your option to switch them off. Do not allow badness set up squatter's rights in your mind. Let my goodness which is all around you flow into your heart and mind. Open your eyes and begin to see my presence in the world. Read the sort of magazine or book that will restore holy consolation to your mind.

Because I love you I come to sit down beside you. Please do not recoil in fear. My presence will bring you peace of spirit and restfulness of mind. My light brings you the truth that will set you free. I have come that you may have life and have it to the full. All you must do is to accept my light, my love and my renewal of life.

Close the meeting with a suitable hymn or prayer.

Unfinished Business

Be quiet and return to inner stillness so that you might be more receptive to the Lord's communication.

 Our prayer is sometimes stunted and withered because of happenings in our past which were never properly cleared up. The business remains unfinished. It is like the tension that affects a relationship when all that needs to be said is never spoken.

Introductory Prayer

O Lord, I find it very hard to be totally relaxed before you. I feel very hypocritical coming to pray while so much resentment and bitterness remain in my heart. My heart is sometimes withered and cold towards certain people. It can just be the way they dress, or their accent or even where they come from. Indeed, sometimes it is plain jealousy that causes the resentment. I am ashamed of jealousy. It is a poisonous parasite that grows out of a good tree. It is a negative reaction to the good fortune or success of others.

Some of my relationships with people are smouldering fires of anger because we have never found the courage to talk things out openly. We are afraid of what might follow once the words begin to flow. We go through the motions of niceness and respectability, but who knows what is buried in the cold silence underneath?

And I have sore memories which I fear will never heal. How can I ever forget what was said and done? How can I obliterate the memory of how I suffered because of selfishness and callous behaviour?. How deeply was I hurt when I was neglected and passed by.

But why must I pour all this out to you, Lord? You already

know me. 'You search me and you know me: you discern my purpose from afar. All my ways lie open to you. Before ever a word is on my tongue, you know it,O Lord, through and through.'

You ask me to reach out to others with hands of forgiveness and with arms of open welcome. But my poor hands are withered. My outreach is limited. I am paralysed by my past.

O Lord, hear my cry. Let my prayer come unto you. Release me from myself. Help me to let go of the chains that shackle me and the blinkers that blind me. Heal my soul of all that is withering that plant of divine love which you planted in me at baptism.

Reflect awhile in silence on the hurts which have limited your love.

A reading from the holy gospel according to Luke (6: 6-11)

On another sabbath Jesus entered the synagogue and began teaching. There was a man with a paralysed hand and the teachers of the law and the Pharisees watched him: Would Jesus heal the man on the sabbath? If he did, they could accuse him.

But Jesus knew their thoughts and said to the man, 'Get up and stand in the middle.' Then he spoke to them, 'I want to ask you: what is allowed by the law on the sabbath, to do good or to do harm, to save life or destroy it?' And Jesus looked around at them all.

Then he said to the man, 'Stretch out your hand.' He stretched it out and his hand was restored, becoming as whole as the other. But they were furious and began to discuss with one another what they could do to Jesus.

First, reflect in silence on what the passage means to you. Then, if you wish, chat among yourselves about the atmosphere of tension that day in the synagogue.

Reflecting on the Word

Central to Luke's story is the statement that Jesus knew their thoughts. On the surface level the story is about a withered hand: but the concern of Jesus is more about withered hearts and blocked minds

Notice how the entire context is religious. The day is the holy day of the week, the place is the holy house and the holy act of teaching is going on. But under that veneer of piety all is not well. Hypocritical piety is often used as a cover up for the heart that is full of bitterness. Jesus experienced far more trouble from so-called religious people than from atheists or scoundrels.

Jesus penetrated their cover for he could read their hearts. He understood their mental blockages and prejudices. He challenged the sincerity of their piety by asking them about their understanding of the law. In that context the law meant the very heart of religion. He asked them was their religion more a source of bitterness than a commitment to goodness. And it still happens, unfortunately, that some Christians are so obsessed with evil that they have no energy left for celebrating the Lord's goodness. Like a team totally obsessed with defence and never trying to score. No wonder people can find church boring!

The words of Jesus to the handicapped man appeal to the imagination: 'Stretch out your hand.' We are invited to picture the bewildered man discovering new muscles in his withered arm, pushing out in stages, further bewildered until the arm is fully extended into an orbit it had never known.

Luke, as is his wont, tells us the reaction of the people to the gracious action of Christ. Sadly, in this instance they are furious and more hardened than before in their bitterness. Instead of hearing Jesus they plotted how to deal with him.

The whole episode challenges us to stand up and face any mental blockages we might have:
Is there anybody you just cannot bring yourself to talk to? *(Pause)*
Is there a relationship which suffers because the air was never cleared after some hurtful experience? *(Pause)*
Are there matters of health and anxiety which you are afraid even to name? *(Pause)*
How long is the business of the past to remain unfinished? *(Pause)*

Let us pray.
Lord, give us the prudence to know when to remain silent and when to confront a situation. Lord, hear us.
Lord, save us from all negative, jealous thoughts about people. Lord, hear us.
May our religious devotion never be hypocritical. Lord, hear us.

Let people have time for their own reflections and prayers.

Jesus replies

O my poor little friend! I know your problems and pains, your hurts and haltings, your fears and failures. I know you through and through. I understand where your problems come from. How you have carried them through the years. How you have let the small wounds fester into a dangerous poison.

It grieves my heart to see your life stunted and your love

withered. How I long to release you and see you stretch out to your potential. Remember the life that you received at baptism. My own life. My own love. It is planted as a seed in you. A seed that must grow and flower.

You must let it grow. You must so desire my love that you will let go of all the negativity. You must stand out from the shadows and let my light shine upon you. Do not be afraid of my light. My light is always full of love. It is a light from my heart, the warm light you get from a fire. Come to the warm light of my heart. You will see and your frozen areas will be thawed out and warmed.

My special message to you tonight is that the truth will set you free. Come to me and be released in the truth of your life. Hide in the shadows no longer. These shadows have stunted your growth and withered your heart. Stand out in the life-giving sunshine of my love. Tell your story to some trusted soul-friend who will pray with you. As you struggle with your words your soul will be set free. I have bestowed on my church the power of forgiveness and the grace of inner healing.

Come then, my friend, to my love. Stand up in total honesty and discover how you can stretch out your love to its potential. Come out from the cold and dark. Open your heart to receive my love. Open your memory to my healing grace. Take my life which I share with you in the Eucharist. Receive your fulness. Grow into your marvellous potential.

Close the meeting with a suitable prayer or hymn.

Growing in the dark

Be quiet and recollected in God's presence for a few minutes.

 Prayer is not always easy. There are times when it is hard to hope or to have courage. Sometimes all the bad news of everyday life really gets in on us. Maybe it is triggered off by anxiety about the way someone we love is behaving. The bad news can close in on us like a cold, clinging fog that blocks out all light and warmth. In this meeting with Jesus we grope towards him out of our experience of darkness in our faith.

Introductory Prayer

O Lord, it is dark. I am feeling very down at the moment. There is no light in my faith, no joy in my prayer. Every ounce of courage is gone. I am so dragged down by the depressing scene around me. It has got in on me.

I believe, Lord, help my unbelief. I believe in your kingdom. I believe in Pentecost. I believe in the Holy Spirit. But I am in darkness now, Lord, I can no longer see. My faith seems unreal. It is there in my brain but it fails to warm my heart. I can say the right words but they sound like empty shells.

What is getting me down is the awful way people are losing touch with our Christian values. I try not to be judgemental, Lord, but I am shocked at the lowering of moral values. It's hard not to be cynical about the standards shown by our politicians. And the anger of the newspapers against the church is very hurtful. Sexual permissiveness is breaking up family life and leading people into deep pain. It is very worrying to see so many of our younger generation blindly stumbling into the jungle of life without meaning.

There are even happenings in your church, Lord, which

leave me sad. It's no longer a distant problem in far off lands. Now it is in my own family circle. Some do not go to Mass. They do not regard the sacrament of marriage as necessary. They have no respect for our traditional beliefs and values. It is hard to keep hoping, Lord. Where is it all leading to?

And yet, Lord, I do not think for one moment that you have forsaken us. I believe in your victory over sin and darkness. I believe that your Spirit is with us. I believe that you are ever with your church. But my faith is dim and I find it so hard to sustain my hope. My soul seems to be totally enveloped by the dark and my prayer is just a blind groping without light. No bird of song lands on my branches.

How long, O Lord, am I to remain an exile from your presence? How long must I wait before I see the sunshine of your smile again? How long before the dawn of light? How long this night, O Lord?

Allow a time of reflection for people to get in touch with their own personal areas of darkness.

A reading from the holy gospel according to Mark (4:26-29)

Jesus also said 'In the kingdom of God it is like this. A man scatters seed upon the soil. Whether he is asleep or awake, be it day or night, the seed sprouts and grows, he knows not how. The soil produces of itself; first the blade, then the ear, then the full grain in the ear. But as soon as the grain is ripe, the man starts cutting it with a sickle, because harvest time has come.'

 *What are your own inspirations or thoughts from this reading?*

Reflecting on the Word

The point we pick up from the parable is how the seed grows through the night as well as in the day. We apply it to the dark experiences in our faith, the times when all around us is night.

The man who planted the seed does not have to understand the biological laws of growth. He does not know how the mystery of growth takes place. But from experience he knows that he must have patience. You do not expect September's apples a week after April's blossoms. In its proper time the field will be ready for harvesting.

Our spiritual growth will not always be in days of light and joy. We experience hardship and losses, defeats and disappointments. If we live through Summer we must also accept Winter. Daylight does not last forever but yields to the blanket of night.

Faith is a dim light. A light that offers much to us regarding the meaning of life and the values we ought to cherish. But it is a dim light because it cannot penetrate some of the inexplicable happenings we meet and endure. We have to accept what St. Paul said of God: that sometimes his ways are unsearchable and his judgments inscrutable.

The parable of Jesus assures us that the seed of the kingdom keeps on growing through the times of darkness and spiritual sleep.

Reflect quietly on your own experiences of darkness, when prayer was a severe struggle. What drags you down from the plateau of joy and hope?

Let us pray:
In our darkness, Lord, may your face shine once more on your servants. Lord, hear us.
Grant us perseverance in our faith and prayer. Lord, hear us.
May we never lose confidence in the presence of the Holy Spirit in the church. Lord, hear us.

Invite people to make their own petitions.

Jesus replies

My dear friend, you know that I am with you. Always with you. Never lose heart. You must accept, though, that sometimes I have to challenge you. Otherwise you will not grow in your faith.

Observe how the earth needs a Winter when things decay so as to strengthen the surge of life in spring. Think how hurtful for your eyes it would be if there were no darkness. Night is restful to your eyes. Your faith needs its times of darkness to make you lengthen your vision. Remember that it is only in the dark of night that you can see the distant stars. You must stretch the vision of your faith to see greater depths of our relationship.

If it were all light and comfort then you might know me as your friend but not as your God. If you could understand everything then your mind would not be ready to accept my mysteries. You would be incapable of any appreciation of the Father's majesty and glory.

My church too needs periods of night and regression. When everything goes well there can be the temptation to be triumphalistic and self-congratulatory. My church must always be humble. And so I permit humiliations to happen for the good of the church. I cannot work with a proud church which does not realise its dependence on me.

My dear friend, I am with you always. Leading you on through the night as much as in the day. And my Blessed Spirit is ever active, bringing little seeds to growth in ways that will surprise you.

The bad news which depresses you dominates the headlines. But why let others do the thinking for you. Open your eyes and see. There are many wonderful people in my church today. There are many people of great generosity and idealism working quietly for my kingdom in the world. The next time you feel overwhelmed by the bad news try to remind yourself of the good that is being done.

My special message to you tonight is to be patient. Have the patience of the farmer who knows that growth takes time.

Whatever happens, have trust.

Trust in me for I am always near.

Trust in the gift of my Spirit. You will have noticed that the Spirit is full of nice surprises. The dawning of light might be nearer than you think.

Finish the meeting with a suitable hymn or prayer.

In times of stress

Invite the group to be quiet for a few minutes. Somebody may lead a prayer to the Holy Spirit to guide your reflections.

Sometimes we come to pray seeking peace from the pressures and stresses of life. We reach out to Jesus for inner strength and peace.

Introductory Prayer

O Lord, you are our refuge and our strength. You are our rock and our salvation. I call out to you as my soul seeks peace from all the pressures building up around me. My soul needs to fly like a bird to its mountain, away from the suffocating air of stress and tension. My soul is longing for your peace.

My body has a language all its own to tell me when the pressure is too much. I know what it is to have the hammers of pressure thudding inside my brain. To have my heart racing and my mind agitated. My tummy acting up and my back aching. My shoulder-blades knotted in a tight ball.

And I can see the signs in others too. Faces drawn tight, lips tense and hard, eyes darting, hands sweaty. There are times when the floodgates open and tempers fly. Voices are loud, words are sharp and attitudes aggressive.

Sometimes we grimly hold back the torrent. But the pressure is there to be seen in bodily tension, communication barriers and a tetchy tone of voice.

Believe me, Lord, but I do try and try very hard. I make the decision that this pressure will not get the better of me. I'll see it through. I remind myself of your suffering, your cross. It helps me to know that you are sharing it with me.

A little secret between us, Lord. I sometimes promise myself a little treat when it is all over. Usually some innocent little treat like a bit of chocolate, or a nice walk. I'm not being too selfish, Lord, am I?

One thing I am very sorry about. The way I give in to self-pity. I see myself as the poor, innocent martyr having to put up with so much because others don't pull their weight. They don't understand my pressures; they are too busy about themselves.

I am feeling a bit better already, Lord. I have calmed down. Talking things out with you always calms me down. Thank you, Lord, and praise you. You are my calm in the storm, my light in the darkness, my oasis in the desert.

Reflect on what stress does to you. What causes pressures to build up in your life?

A reading from the holy gospel according to Mark (1:32-38)

That evening just as the sun had set, people brought to Jesus all the sick and those who had evil spirits. The whole town was gathered near the door. Jesus healed many who had various diseases, and drove out many demons; but he did not let them speak, for they knew who he was.

Very early in the morning, before daylight, Jesus got up and went away to a lonely place where he prayed. Simon and the others went out, too, searching for him; and when they found him they said, 'Everyone is looking for you.' Then Jesus answered, 'Let's go to the nearby villages so that I may preach there also; for that is why I came.'

Among yourselves discuss the pressures on Jesus and what he did to cope with them.

Reflecting on the Word

Mark's gospel is no place for anybody who suffers from claustrophobia. People ... the whole town ... are crowding around the door. The air is suffocating. It is bedlam with people pushing, elbowing, pulling, resisting, clamouring for attention. How self-assertive and hurtful people can be on their way to the Lord!

We note that it was after sunset. One would feel entitled to quietness and rest after the work of the day. But Jesus has become a victim to his own success. His legitimate privacy is being invaded and overrun. He does not want to become an object of curiosity, not a big name celebrity. That sort of chat-show status would be an obstacle to his true mission.

Simon Peter, an extravert if ever there was one, thinks he has great news for Jesus: 'Everybody is looking for you!' But Jesus shuns that sort of publicity. So he moved off to other places and other people.,

The causes of stress in our lives are many and varied. Sometimes, like Jesus in this instance, we are torn apart by the insistent demands of people. Or the work-load increases to the point where it has usurped our time for family, for relaxation, for fun and the celebration of life.

The clock is often the tyrant. Deadlines to be met. Annoying delays and postponements. Anxious waiting. Fretful tossing through the night until the alarm sounds the call to further action. It's not the clock's fault, of course. The stress is within myself.

Sometimes the pressure comes when I cannot cope with the intrusions of others into my space. Visitors put in on my routine. Noisy revellers on the street upset my sleep. Some confrontation or roughness with another lives on for hours... for weeks or months in strained feelings.

One feels it is necessary to keep going and to pretend that everything is fine. Daily life is then a dam which is holding back a dark and deep lake, a backlog of unidentified problems, vague fears, niggling insecurities, unresolved conflicts or unaccepted failures. The lake rises under flood. How long can the restraining wall hold out?

There are many ways recommended for coping with the stresses of life. What did Jesus do in his stressful situation? He accepted morning. It was a new day. So he got up early. There is often a tiredness which is not solved by more sleep but by a new attitude. One must see the morning as offering new possibilities. Jesus left that place.

Pressure from crowds had been at the root of his problem so he wisely sought the compensating opposite: he went off to a lonely place.

We note that there he prayed. In prayer we are uplifted in mind and heart. We reach a higher plane where we can transcend our pressures, fears, insecurities and conflicts. In this bigger vision we see more of the total picture of life and the little parts are then less threatening.

And, above all, in Christian prayer we grow in awareness of God's ever-present love and providence. We receive the divine gift of hope.

Let us pray.
O Lord, as we meet you in prayer, grant us the serenity to cope with the pressures of life. Lord, hear us.
May we always have the good sense to live a balanced life. Lord, hear us.
May our presence never be the cause of tension for others, but, rather, a source of peace. Lord, hear us.

Invite people to add their own thoughts and prayers.

Jesus replies

(Before reading on, pause for a while with your own message from Jesus)

My good friend, thanks for coming to me in your pains and pressures. I know what you are talking about. I have been in your situation. When I shared in your flesh and blood I shared in your stresses and tensions.

You trusted me with your little secret. Now I have a personal message for you. Love yourself.

Make sure that you love yourself and care for yourself. How can you love others if you do not love and respect yourself.

Love your own company. Learn how rich and important you are. You are the precious creation of Our Father. You are the blessed temple of the Holy Spirit. You were loved by me unto the cross.

You need time alone to appreciate all that you are. There is too much noise all around you and too much pressure inside you. You owe it to yourself to get up, to step into a new attitude, to go to your alone-place and there find your richness.

You will discover that you are never alone.

For I am with you. And I love you.

Close the meeting with an appropriate hymn or prayer.

In God's delays

Let everybody relax in quietness as a preparation for prayer. Then invoke the help of the Holy Spirit.

Sometimes it is hard to keep going in the life of faith. We get tired, we lose heart, we get no answers back and we see no signs to excite us. It seems that God is delaying his coming to us.

Introductory Prayer

O Lord, I am a creature of fits and starts. I've known times of great enthusiasm and days when I had to drag myself to prayer. At the moment, Lord, I feel very much on the downward slope.

I thank you for all the bearers of your light who have helped me by their words and example. My life has not been without its share of inspiration and support.

I thank you for our little group, our community of believers who regularly keep me going. Some nights maybe the only consolation I get is the very challenge to come out and meet them. Even if nothing else comes my way, I know that it is good to have stepped out of my self-pity to make the effort to meet them.

There are times when I am very aware of your Holy Spirit praying within me. Everything pours out so easily. It comes in flowing words and it comes beyond the meaning of words. I feel physically warm at your touch. Then I know a little of how your three chosen disciples felt at the transfiguration.

But then comes the desert. Some of your great saints wrote

about the nights of prayer, the times of darkness in faith. I am not suggesting that my experience is a deep as theirs. But it is dark nonetheless.

What tries me most, dear Lord, are the prayers I have offered for years and years for the good of others, but I see no improvement. For the rehabilitation of an alcoholic. For somebody's return to the ways of Christian living. For someone to believe in the Blessed Eucharist. I know that St. Monica prayed for many years before her son, Augustine, broke free from the deceits that entangled him. How long, O Lord, must I keep going?

You have promised us, Lord Jesus, that prayers offered to the Father in your name will be granted. I have prayed in your sacred name. But I still await your answer.

'Ask and you will be given. Seek and you will find. Knock and the door will be opened.' I have taken your words to heart, Lord. I have asked, I have sought and I have knocked. Not once but many times. Yet I see no answer. When will you come to smile on me?

Dear Lord, my faith is sorely tried.

Allow time for private reflection

A reading from the holy gospel according to Luke (18:1-8)

Jesus told them a parable to show them that they should pray continually and not lost heart. He said, 'In a certain town there was a judge who neither feared God nor people. In the same town was a widow who kept coming to him, saying: 'Defend my rights against my opponent.' For a time he refused, but finally he thought: 'Even though I neither fear

God nor care about people, this widow bothers me so much I will see that she gets justice; then she will stop coming and wearing me out.'

And Jesus explained, 'Listen to what the evil judge says. Will God not do justice for his chosen ones who cry to him day and night even if he delays in answering them? I tell you, he will speedily do them justice. Yet, when the Son of Man comes, will he find faith on earth?'

Chat among yourselves about the teaching of Jesus on persevering in prayer. And what did he say about God delaying an answer?

Reflecting on the Word

In this parable Jesus encourages two great qualities in our prayerlife. Our prayer must be continual and we should never lose heart or hope.

Our prayer must be continual. God's relationship with us suffers no breaks in continuity. We would immediately disintegrate unless God were reaching out to us 365 days of the year, sharing life, light and love with us every moment of the day. A life of prayer means every day responding to this God who is reaching out towards us. Remembering God who has given us this day. Adoring the Lord of all majesty. Loving the God who loves each one of us with a very personal love. Thanking God for the gift of every breath and heartbeat. Asking God for what we need. Repenting of our failures, weaknesses and sins.

Continual prayer is a daily ALTAR of adoration, love, thanks, asking and repenting.

But in times of darkness or fatigue it can be hard to keep going. So, the second teaching of Jesus is about not losing heart. People find that the very times they most need prayer are when they find it hardest: in times of illness or depression, in the loneliness after a bereavement, in the inner brokenness that follows sin. It is some consolation to remember that other people are praying for you at these times.

The advice of St. Paul for the times when we cannot find words is to hand over everything to the Holy Spirit who has been given to us at baptism. Invite the Holy Spirit to make a prayer out of every sigh from your sad heart, from every silent tear you shed, from every pain you feel. Each pain or sigh or tear is but an expression of your emptiness. And your emptiness only gives more space to God in your soul. When the Holy Spirit develops your faith you will understand that God is using pain to stretch your capacity ... like stretching a bag to make it hold more.

The parable says that God sometimes delays his answer. Whatever God wills for us comes from his love. Even his delays are motivated by love. If ever we feel drowning in a sea of dark doubts we have the words of Jesus to hold onto like a saving raft: 'Will not God see justice done to his chosen who cry to him day and night even when he delays to help them?'

If God chooses to delay in answering us, that's okay. God's answer will come in God's way and at God's time. And God's time is the best time.

'When the Son of Man comes, will he find faith on earth?' A startling question. What Jesus is referring to is fidelity: that unsinkable sort of trust that God loves us, no matter how messed about and tortured our circumstances may be.

We are to ask ourselves do we return time to God in prayer every day. Many times every day? Have I patience with God's time? Am I so deeply convinced of God's love that I totally trust in his care and his timing? Or do I insist on my view of things? Do I abandon everything into God's hands?

Let us pray.
Lord, may we respect your delays as much as we rejoice in your coming. Lord, hear us.
Grant us a great willingness to let the Holy Spirit take over in our prayer. Lord, hear us.
May we remain faithful to you at all times. Lord, hear us.

Allow time for personal petitions.

Jesus replies

My dear child in faith. Know that I love you. Know it in every cell of your being that I love you. I will never desert you or let you down. You desire to know me and to share your life with me. But it is not enough that you should share the joys of the wedding at Cana and the sure conviction of the light on the mountain. You must also share something of my agony in Gethsemane.

Your faith must bear with testing. I do not test you in the cruel sense of seeing how far you can go without breaking. My testing is a way of drawing out your faith to a deeper fulfilment. My testing is love's way of asking you to grow.

I need to stretch your vision. Remember that it is only in the dark of night that your eyesight stretches to the distant stars. In the light of day your eyes are totally filled by what is very near about you. In the same way, your prayers too often come out of a very limited view. Your vision needs to be stretched out to greater horizons.

I also need to stretch the desire of your heart. You know how a garment after washing may need to be stretched before you fit it on again. By delaying my answer to your prayers I am but stretching the desire of your heart.

I do not wish to spoil you like parents who cannot refuse their children anything. Let them make but one whimper and the parent gives in. The child is spoiled and never learns patience or the appreciation of the free nature of a gift. If every prayer were granted to you without delay you would be left with a very shallow faith. You would befriend me for what you could get out of me. You would make use of me for selfish purposes.

I long to see your faith freed of selfishness. I wish to draw you to a more pure faith which takes nighttime as calmly as daylight, winter as well as summer.

But always be sure that your every prayer reaches my heart. Trust me. Trust the wisdom of my delays. Trust my timing. Your patience in prayer will show the depth of your trust in me.

I love you with an everlasting love which reaches far beyond instant answers. I love you in a way that calls you to grow in your faith, to add length to your vision, to deepen your desiring.

Seek me, but do not limit your search to your own expectations.

Seek me, trusting that all I do for you is full of love.

Close the meeting with a suitable prayer or hymn.

In times of negativity

Be quiet and still to prepare for prayer. Somebody may then lead in a suitable preparatory prayer.

In this meeting with Jesus we open our hearts to take in all those who are going through a very dark period and are very negative about their self-worth. Nothing will drag us down so quickly as a low sense of self-esteem.

Prayer from the pits

O Lord, I am drained. Dead inside. I must have no faith. I cannot pray any more.

Somebody passed by and she was singing that song, 'Any dream will do.' I felt she was singing it at me. I am so locked up in myself that I am removed from reality. Life is all a dream. I find myself reaching out to touch a chair or a table just to see is it real. My faith is all a dream. When I think I have faith I grasp at it and it is gone. Like grasping at a mist. Or trying to recapture a dream.

Lord, is there any reality, anything I can touch and hold on to? Or is my own dark thinking the only world that I will ever contact?

Out of the depths I cry to you O Lord.

Prayer of an exhausted soul

Lord, I am shattered. When you asked me to witness before others I couldn't refuse. I felt unworthy and afraid but it was such a privilege to be called that I accepted. I trusted in your help.

How I got through it I do not know. Sorry, Lord, but I do

know. You pulled me through it. But nobody could have suspected all that was happening inside me.

On the outside, I got through everything. I survived. I acted the part. But inside! I never felt so empty and on my own. So lonely.

I am totally drained now, Lord. I have wept and wept for two whole days. There's nothing left inside. Where is your angel of comfort in my agony? I am so empty, so shattered, so broken to pieces. Will I ever again have peace? Will I ever again be able to face the world?

Prayer of a tired priest

O Lord, be merciful to me a sinner. I must be the world's greatest hypocrite. I stand at the altar in your name while I shudder inside from my unworthiness. I'm so empty inside, drained, exhausted. There was a time when I was excited by faith. But now everything is flat and dead.

I struggle to face others, to smile and cheer them. I have to encourage others when I have no courage myself. I have to drag myself to preach your good news while I find nothing inspiring me. Whenever anybody praises my effort, it only increases my feeling of being a hypocrite.

I give all the right advice to others but I contradict it in my own life. If they only knew what I am like behind the pious exterior!

My only consolation is when I think of what happened to you, Lord. You were crucified for your efforts. And you cried out in pain of the spirit 'My God, my God, why have you forsaken me.'

Crucified Jesus, crying Jesus, Jesus of the split-open heart, help me to survive.

You might like to say if these prayers touched your own experience ... or the experiences of people you care about.

A reading from the holy gospel according to Luke (12:24-28)

Look at the crows: they neither sow nor reap; they have no storehouses and no barns; yet God feeds them. How much more important are you than birds! Which of you for all his worrying can make himself a little taller? And if you are not able to control such a small thing, why do you worry about the rest?

Look at the wild flowers: they do not spin or weave; yet I tell you, even Solomon with all his wealth was not clothed as one of these. But if God so clothes the grass in the fields, which is alive today and tomorrow is thrown into the oven, how much more will he clothe you, people of little faith.

Are you consoled and uplifted by these words of Jesus? Do you sense your great value in the eyes of God?

Reflecting on the Word

Jesus encourages us to think positively about our value before God. If the flowers and the birds are of so much value in God's providence, then how much more are we!

Jesus knew our tendency to go into the downward spiral of negative thinking. Like all the worrying that produces nothing. And all the anxiety that is caused by those matters which are outside our control. Sometimes it can be a very small matter which triggers off our plunge into negativity. Or we get upset because something is not totally perfect.

Put these questions to yourself and see if you are too hasty in knocking yourself. Do you let one small imperfection in a job or situation upset your satisfaction at what you have achieved?

Do you generalise after a failure ... 'Oh, but I am always failing that way ... sure, I'm a born loser.'

When somebody praises your accomplishment, do you find it hard to accept the praise? Do you defend yourself from affirmation by mentioning the bit that went wrong, or the chance that you missed?

Are you always anticipating criticism from others? Are you under constant pressure to compare yourself with others and come off the loser in the comparison?

Do you feel that you have never done anything to deserve the love of others? Do you find it hard to believe that God could possibly love you after all you've done in the past?

Jesus encourages us to open our eyes and think positively. Stop going inwards into an unhealthy darkness. Open your eyes to the wonders of life ... in the unglamorous crow, the little flower, the blade of grass, the intricacy of the leaf, the age of the stone, the mystery of the shell. See the precious construction in that humble object. And take to heart the words of the Lord – 'How much more are you worth!'

Let us pray.

Lord, may we learn wisdom from contemplating the mysteries of nature all around us. Lord, hear us.

May our belief in your support overcome all our self-doubting. Lord, hear us.

Teach us how to thank you daily for the wonder of our being. Lord, hear us.

Allow time for personal reflections and prayers.

Jesus replies
(First spend a little while in silence reflecting on what thoughts or inspiration you may have received from God.)
My dear children, how my own agonies on earth are continuing in you today! I want you to let go of all these negative feelings which are spoiling your lives.

GATHER IN MY NAME

I cannot repeat it too often for you: do not be afraid. You are very precious in my eyes.

Please stop knocking yourself. Remember that when you are knocking yourself you are insulting our Father who fashioned you. For when you were made he rubbed his hands in satisfaction and said 'It is good, very good.' Very good, for you are made in the divine image and likeness. You have been made with a deep capacity for heaven and divine life. The dissatisfactions you feel here on earth are part of that huge emptiness which only the life of heaven will ever fill.

Please try to love yourself. Remember how much I have loved you. I loved you unto the cross. Love yourself enough to give up all that is harming you.

Here is my special message to you this evening. It comes in three steps:

First, stop all that unhealthy self-analysis which is only leaving you deflated and depressed.

Second, open your eyes to see the wonders of reality all about you. Like I said before, see the birds of the sky, see the flower, see any single object and focus on it for a while. Contemplate on its colour, its shape. Has it a smell? What is its purpose or usefulness? How long is its lifespan? Enter into the mystery of any living creature. Let it minister to you. Let it draw you out of yourself. I have painted my world with beauty so that your thoughts might be lifted up and healed. And be open to surprises, for I spread many little surprise gifts on your road every day ... if only you would open your eyes to notice them.

The third step is to keep on blessing and praising your heavenly Father. Even if you are in sin, do not stop praising and blessing. You may not feel like doing it, but do it nonetheless. Praise God in the storm. Praise God in the desert. Praise God in the emptiness. Praise God in time of temptation.

You are of great value. Live up to what the Father has given to you and in that way, live unto the praise of his glory. Let your life be a living word of praise.

Close the meeting with a suitable hymn or blessing.

Bruised and betrayed

Settle in silence for a while to open up your mind and heart to God. Then humbly ask God for the grace of prayer.

 Is there any personal hurt more severe than the pain of being betrayed in trust and love? The love we have received is our greatest source of inner strength in life. If this source is poisoned by betrayal, it is an injury to the very backbone of life. It is hard to stand up or to face others with any confidence. Our prayer this evening comes out of the experience of bruising and betrayal.

Introductory Prayer

Lord, how I envy those who can stand up and speak out in total confidence. They look so relaxed and secure in themselves. I can usually manage to say some words but these are only sounds to fill an empty space. Words that carry nothing of the real me. Words of no sharing, for I can no longer trust anybody in total security.

I feel I have been hurt too often to have confidence. My personal secrets have been carried to ears that had no right to hear them. My personal life has been exposed. My mind is always worried by what others might be thinking about me. No matter how I dress I am always left with the thought that I should have put on something else. Even when people compliment me I fear that they are secretly laughing at me and mocking me.

I always feel under pressure in the crowd at church as I keep thinking that every eye is on me. Like television cameras at every angle. Coming back from Holy Communion is the longest walk I ever experience.

Those I thought I could trust have let me down. I've had too many fair weather friends who never had the time when I really needed them.

Being honest with you, Lord, I must confess that I have not always been a faithful friend either. I find that I am not always open and honest with people at home. Since I do not trust them, why should I expect them to trust me? So, I am not always fully open or truthful with them. Trust is a two-way operation. Unfortunately, infidelity also tends to be two-way. Having experienced unfaithfulness, I tend to be unfaithful too.

O God, my rock, my foundation, how my bleeding heart cries out to you! My confused mind yearns for total trust and understanding. My shattered life longs for that peace of having all the parts drawn together into one. My betrayed heart thirsts for healing at the well of your love.

Pause to reflect on how love was betrayed and confidence shattered ... in your own life or for people close to you.

A reading from the holy gospel according to John (Chap. 4)

Jesus came to a Samaritan town called Sychar, near the land that Jacob had given to his son Joseph. Jacob's well is there. Tired from his journey, Jesus sat down by the well: it was about noon. Now a Samaritan woman came to draw water and Jesus said to her, 'Give me a drink.' His disciples had just gone into town to buy some food.

The Samaritan woman said to him, 'How is it that you, a Jew, ask me, a Samaritan and a woman, for a drink?' (For Jews, in fact, have no dealings with Samaritans.) Jesus replied, 'If you only knew the Gift of God! If you knew who it is that asks you for a drink, you yourself would have asked me and I would have given you living water.'

The woman answered, 'Sir, you have no bucket and this well is deep; where is your living water? Are you greater than our ancestor Jacob, who gave us this well after he drank from it himself, together with his children and his cattle?'

Jesus said to her, 'Whoever drinks of this water will be thirsty again; but whoever drinks of the water that I shall give will never be thirsty; for the water that I shall give will become in him a spring of water welling up to eternal life.'

The woman said to him, 'Give me this water, that I may never be thirsty and never have to come here to draw water.' Jesus said, 'Go, call your husband and come back here.' The woman answered, 'I have no husband.' And Jesus replied, 'You are right to say: 'I have no husband'; for you have had five husbands and the one you have now is not your husband. What you said is true' ... The woman said to him, 'I know that the Messiah, that is the Christ, is coming; when he comes, he will tell us everything.' And Jesus said, 'I who am talking to you, I am he.'

So the woman left her water jar and ran to the town. Then she said to the people, 'Come and see a man who told me everything I did! Could he not be the Christ?'

How did the woman feel about God before she met Jesus? How did she feel after their meeting? Can you associate your own life with this story?

Reflecting on the Word

This is the story of a lonely woman with a very bruised heart. She had been betrayed in religion for, in her experience, it only set people at emnity with one another. The God of love and understanding was unknown to her.

Nor had she fared any better in human relationships. Five

GATHER IN MY NAME

marriages, but not one of them survived. 'I have no husband,' she said. She had experienced so much hurt and betrayal that she was no longer capable of saying 'forever' to any man. 'True,' said Jesus compassionately, 'and the one you have now is no husband.'

The gospel notes that it was the sixth hour, midday, a time of day when people usually stayed in the shade to avoid the excessive heat. It was also unusual that she came alone to the well. In a society where women had virtually no opportunity for contact in public, the daily visit to the well was the highlight of the day. It seems that this woman was coming alone as she was not accepted by the others because of her multiple affairs.

Betrayed in religion, bruised in love and socially outcast, she met Jesus at the well. She was deeply moved by Jesus: moved on a level she had never previously experienced.

She is quickly aware that he is a religious man. And that he is speaking of a thirst much deeper than physical. Her empty, betrayed heart is excited by what he has to offer. She knows it is on the religious level for she mentions the promised Messiah ... 'and when he comes he will teach us everything.' Perhaps in her lonely hours she had longed for this Messiah who might make sense of religion and offer hope to the likes of herself.

Imagine her joy when Jesus tells her that he is the promised one. See her run back into the town. She is no longer afraid to face the people. She calls them to come out and meet Jesus. 'He told me everything I ever did!' Everything? Well, hardly. But at least she felt so totally understood and accepted that every hidden detail was included. The lonely soul had found its fountain of living water.

Let us pray

O Lord, our souls too thirst for your love, understanding and mercy. Lord, hear us.

May we find delight in the fountains of the Holy Spirit in our souls. Lord, hear us.

Grant forgiveness to all who have betrayed or hurt our love. Lord, hear us.

Allow time for your own thoughts and prayers to be expressed.

Jesus replies

Dear friend, be not afraid. Here, take a seat beside me. Trust me and relax a little. Away with those barriers you are so quick to erect around yourself.

I have seen each and every bruise that life has ministered to you. I have watched you drawing back at each disappointment, your heart forming a hard, defensive shell with every betrayal. I know and understand all that you have been through.

Have you forgotten that I too was betrayed, misunderstood and rejected. Even my close disciples deserted me in my hour of greatest need. So, my friend, you are not alone in your experience of betrayal.

At the well of Sychar, do you remember that I asked my friend there for her bucket? It was important that she had something I did not possess, something she could give me.

And I want something from you too. There is something you must do for me. Lend me your bucket by opening up the capacity of your heart to receive my love. Come out from behind that hard shell for just a moment.

For too long you have suffered deeply because you have closed yourself off. You have tried to hide away from life and love. You have ever been before my eyes hiding in silence, wearing hard masks to cover your softness, posing as somebody you are not.

Just be yourself. Accept yourself. I do not ask you to be anybody else. It is you that I love. Let me come to you and help you.

Open up your heart and discover what a wealth you have

inside. Do you know who is in your heart? From your baptism my Holy Spirit has been resting in your heart. All the while you were weak though the source of strength was within you. All the times your love was disappointed though the Spirit of divine love was resting in you. All the nights you yearned for someone to understand you though the Spirit of consolation was there with you.

Tonight, then, tell the Holy Spirit that you are sorry for your years of neglecting his presence. And let go of every barrier which you have used to defend yourself from the outside world and its hurts. Sadly, this same defensive shell cut you off from your own inner heart and from the Spirit within you.

Your deepest thirst will be satisfied by the waters of the Spirit, a fountain of living water in your baptised soul. Come to meet me at the well every day and sit down beside me. Meet me in a quiet church ... or in your favourite chair ... or in reading the word of the bible. All I need from you is the bucket of your emptiness that I might fill it with my Spirit of love.

Finish the meeting with an appropriate hymn or prayer.

Come apart

Prepare for prayer with a period of quietness. Then ask the Holy Spirit to come to your aid.

 As the pressures of life get in on us and deprive us of inner serenity, we feel the need to get away and to be alone with the Lord for awhile. In this meeting with Jesus we tell him of how we are torn apart in our inmost beings.

Introductory Prayer

O Lord, I must be close to breaking point. The pressures keep mounting up. I keep on slogging away but I am totally empty inside. I am so caught up in all that I have to do that I have no energy left for inner work.

I must confess, Lord, that I find it very hard to slow down and sit in peace. It is so true, indeed, that work keeps expanding to the amount of time available to it. There is never free time unless we decide to make it. What happens is that the trivial details grow ever more important. It's the non essentials that multiply and expand. The really important things of life and spirit get squeezed out.

So, Lord, when I come to pray, the OFF switch does not function for me. The world follows me into prayer. It invades my mind. As soon as I take out a book or the beads, or try to reflect, my mind is invaded by the 101 things still to be done.

Prayer equals distractions. I'm afraid that's my story, Lord. Yet I must praise and thank you for leading me to our little prayer-group. They support my prayer more than they suspect. I have found new strength in this community of faith.

GATHER IN MY NAME

Sometimes I have gone to this group with the weight of the world on my shoulders only to have it lifted off by the prayer around me. Truly, Lord, wherever two or three gather in your name you are with them.

Not that we are perfect as a group. I still cannot totally relax or let go of everything. We have our little sensitivities and unspoken annoyances. Sometimes I find myself blocked by the fear of what others might be thinking about me. I cannot be sure but they might not like something I'd like to say. And that fear still holds me back.

So, help me to relax more, Lord. Help me to let go of my pressure, my anxieties and my fears. Grant me a mind at rest and a soul at peace that I might praise you with all my heart and soul and mind.

Members of the group may share on what puts pressure on their lives: what tears them apart: what crowds out their inner space.

A reading from the holy gospel according to Mark (6:30-32)

The apostles returned and reported to Jesus all that they had done and taught. Then he said to them, 'Go off by yourselves to a remote place that you may have some rest.' For there were so many people coming and going that the apostles had no time even to eat. And they went away in the boat to a secluded area by themselves.

Spend a while with your own reflections on this invitation of Jesus. When have you found restfulness by coming away? Where do you relax your tension ... with nature, in a quiet chapel, with music ... any other way?

Reflecting on the Word

This passage moves from intense activity to the inner rest-fulness of enjoying the Lord's company undisturbed. It is about returning from the work of the Lord to the Lord of the work.

Interestingly, this is the only place where St. Mark refers to the close band of followers as apostles, a name which implies being sent out on active mission. Perhaps Mark is keen to show that the heart of the apostolate is the apostolate of the heart. 'Apart from me you can do nothing.'

There were many people coming and going, touching on their lives, stealing their personal space, tearing them apart. When we are torn apart by others' demands then it is time to come apart in search of rest. Hence the invitation of Jesus to come away to some place removed from the pressure points. A little group who gather to pray with Jesus resemble the apostles with him in the boat.

Notice how the gospel says that they went away to a secluded place by themselves. The focus is on caring for the inner self. Many busy people neglect this ministry to their own hearts. They feel they must be continually answering the needs of others to prove their self-worth. They depend too much on drawing affirmation from others.

The Lord calls us to stop doing for awhile. To stop ministering to others so as to attend to our inner selves. To be oneself. Observe what is happening in oneself. Within the family.

And to be with God. Attentive to where God has been leading me and touching my life.

We are called by Jesus to venture into these times of deliberate inactivity so as to be alone with God. Then we discover that being alone can be changed from the emptiness of loneliness to the fulness of solitude.

Solitude is chosen for the delight of being alone with the Great Alone.

Let us pray.
O Lord, teach us how to let go of the pressures of life and how to be quiet with you in prayer. Lord, hear us.

May we learn the delights of prayer and recognise our need to come apart with you. Lord, hear us.
Deepen our inner restfulness so that we might draw others to pray. Lord, hear us.

Invite members to add their own prayers or thoughts.

Jesus replies

O my dear, troubled and anxious friends, how I wish to set your souls at peace. That is why I invite you to come away from the pressures. Come to a place of quietness where your faith is nurtured. Come and relax your spirit with me. Come and find rest.

Leave behind all the pain and the anger over what happened during the day. Let go also of your anxious fretting about the future which will come only in its own good time. Sufficient for the moment is my invitation to rest. Enjoy my being with you.

I am with each one of you as a person precious in my eyes. I am with you as a group gathered in my name. So, let everything go and focus on my presence with you.

I know you have distractions and group sensitivities. Distracting thoughts are bound to come, given the nature of your mind. Don't be bothered about them. Don't give them too much importance by battling with them. Smile inwardly at them. They are part of your own life, your own memories. That is why I say smile at these parts of yourself. And pass from them to focus on my presence with you.

Focus on my words in the bible. Listen attentively to them. Read them over and over until they come alive within you, touching your experiences, triggering off your thoughts. Search for a word or a phrase that will be my light for you. I always have some light, some personal message for you. You will appreciate my message better when you have to search for it or wait in patience.

Let my words lift you up beyond all the frettings you have brought in with you. Let my words transcend the petty agitations of spirit which tear you apart in body, mind and spirit.

Come, dear friends, come apart on a regular basis. Come away from the pressure points to find rest for your souls.

Come and find that I am with you ... with you always, even when you are not aware of my presence.

Close your meeting with a prayer of thanksgiving.

In sinfulness

Prepare in silence before inviting the help of the Holy Spirit.

 It is important to know that we can meet Jesus in our sinfulness. It is in time of sin, weakness and temptation that we need to meet Jesus more than ever. Our inclination might be to turn and run away until we are good enough to face God. The beautiful message of the gospel is all about God coming in search of lost sheep and struggling souls.

Introductory Prayer

O Lord, tonight I can hardly talk to you at all. My soul is so tired, I am weighed down. It is hard to go any further.

Sometimes I think it would be easier if I had no conscience, if I did not believe in you at all, if I never had to face you, never had to pray. I know that's a terrible thing to say. I'm sorry, Lord, but that's how low I am feeling right now.

I have fallen again. Gone back to my old ways. I was getting on grand for a time. Now it is such a let down. Such a disappointment with myself. I am cold and empty inside. I struggle to show a presentable face to others.

I read that Job wished he had never been born. I can understand how he felt so low. The only memory that keeps me afloat is the memory of your love for sinners.

As I talk with you now, Lord, I find I must have some spark of hope left. At least I have the courage now to come to you. But I still hide behind my hands and I am too ashamed to look you in the eye.

The more I think of your mercy, the more guilty I feel. For I have presumed on your forgiveness. I have abused the privilege of your love.

O Lord, how I wish I could let go now in a flood of tears like Magdalen or Peter. Tears of relief, tears of washing, tears of new life.

In my lowly state I abandon myself to your love. There is no other refuge for me, no other source of hope, no other home to take me in.

Lord, may my disappointment drive me to depend even more on your help. May my shame serve to establish me in humility. May the extent of my guilt be all the more reason for your mercy to triumph.

Lord Jesus Christ, have mercy on me a weak and broken sinner.

Lord Jesus Christ, I abandon myself totally to your cleansing mercy.

Allow time for personal reflection. When you are aware of your sinfulness, do you want to hide from God or do you turn to him in humble prayer?

A reading from the holy gospel according to Luke (15:1-7)

Meanwhile tax collectors and sinners were seeking the company of Jesus, all of them eager to hear what he had to say. But the Pharisees and scribes frowned at this, muttering. 'This man welcomes sinners and eats with them.' So Jesus told them this parable.

'Who among you, if he has a hundred sheep and loses one of them, will not leave the ninety-nine in the wilderness and seek out the lost one till he finds it? And finding it, will he not joyfully carry it home on his shoulders. Then he will call his friends and neighbours together and say: 'Celebrate with me for I have found my lost sheep.' I tell you, just so, there

GATHER IN MY NAME

will be more rejoicing in heaven over one repentant sinner than over ninety-nine upright who do not need to repent.'

Spend some time with your own thoughts from the reading. Does God want us to hide in the cold and dark after we have strayed?

Reflecting on the Word

The evangelist Luke loved to emphasize the unbroken faithfulness of God's love for us. God remains totally loving towards us even when we are unfaithful to our promises. There is no ON/OFF switch on God's love: not even a dimmer switch. God's love is not conditioned by whether we are being good or not. It is never less than one hundred per cent.

Jesus brought an extraordinary revolution into religious thinking. The prevailing thinking went along the lines that religion was for good-living, virtuous people. But Jesus brought in the notion that religion is really for sinful people. And the church he founded was designed with sinners in mind.

The scribes and Pharisees frowned on the ways of Jesus. Even today there are Abundant Life Seminars where speakers claim that success in business is a reward from God for virtuous living. That is the theory of the God of the Cadillac, totally at variance with Christ of the gospel.

If we were very good-living people we would not really need the church. It is because we are weak that we need the support of others in our faith. We come to pray with others, not because we are tops at prayer, but because we need support and help. We need a system such as the sacraments to celebrate the companionship of Jesus at the most important moments of life's journey.

Those who reject the church because of the obvious human failings of church members have got it all wrong. Jesus shocked and scandalised the religious people of his day by the way he welcomed sinners and went to table with them. He wants sinners to come to his table ... and to his church.

In the parable of the lost sheep we note that the shepherd went after the stray. When we go astray on the ways of sin the biggest mistake would be to panic or to run into frantic diversion or activity. The secret is to stay still because the Good Shepherd will come looking for us. And to quieten our minds so that we might hear his call.

We also note the amount of rejoicing when the lost sheep is found. If the ordinary joy of heaven comes from seeing the goodness of saintly people, then heaven's extraordinary moment of joy is at the repentance of a sinner. What a privilege to be able to add to the joy of heaven!

Jesus called for a celebration of repentance. That is why the church recognises a special sacrament of reconciliation. The reason for confession is not to read out an itemised list of sins to God. He already knows that list better than we do. The reason for a sacrament is the need to celebrate what God's mercy does for us.

Let us pray
Merciful Lord, you are the Good Shepherd who searches for the one who strays. May we deeply appreciate your mercy so that we never lose heart. Lord, hear us.

May we never abuse your mercy so as to presume on your forgiveness. But may the thought of your love strengthen our resolve not to sin again. Lord, hear us.

We pray for all sinners: that they have the grace to come to their senses and to return to their Father's house. Lord, hear us.

Let people have time to reflect and to add their own prayers.

GATHER IN MY NAME

Jesus replies

Beloved child of my heart, could you but know how I bled for you in your sin and your loss of hope! See how I went into anguish with you in Gethsemane. Look at my heart physically pierced and spiritually pouring out to you: rivers of cleansing water and torrents of life-giving blood.

The moment you strayed away from me I missed you. Did you know that? There are millions in my flock but I know each one by name. And I missed you.

I called out your name but you had gone out of reach. The more you gave in to panic and darkness, the further you had gone from my voice. But all the time I was following you. If I moved too soon it would have frightened you all the more. So I had to come gently until you broke down in humble prayer. One humble plea for mercy and I was able to reach out to you and put you on my shoulder.

I come with no rod of punishment. But I do offer you some words of correction. You must realise that you have to stand firm against the wiles of the evil one. The tempter will try to confuse your mind and tantalise your imagination with forbidden fruit. You must not let yourself be mislead.

Now, dear lost child, come to me. Remember my invitation to all who labour and are heavily burdened. I promise to give you rest. Return to the memory of my love for sinners as the evangelists have recorded it. Come before the crucifix which is my own book of love, written not in ink but in the very blood from my heart. Come to me in quietness and trust. Then you will find your strength restored.

Above all come to me in the sacrament of mercy. Do not feel burdened by the need to compile a dossier of sins. I know them already better that you do yourself. I want you to come with a humble heart, open to all I desire to give you.

If you are familiar with the gospel you must know that there is nothing I relish more than an excuse for a celebration! So come and let us celebrate mercy in the sacrament of the church.

Closing prayer or blessing.

In time of storm

Relax in quietness and ask the guidance of the Holy Spirit.

 This evening we come to pray out of the storms of life. We turn to the gospel scene of the apostles' boat on the stormy sea. The boat represents the Church caught up in the turmoil of to-day. In this era of rapid change and constant criticism, people are finding it hard to have courage.

Introductory Prayer

O distant God, where are you? Why have you gone so far away? My soul is a boat cut loose on a stormy sea. I have lost all safe anchorage. There seems to be nothing to hold on to.

I am dragged down in spirit by all the bad news around us. Society seems to be collapsing about us. The moral backbone of society is under constant attack. Those who defend it are ridiculed. Permissive ways are glorified. The media are fascinated by scandals. Little wonder that many marriages are breaking down and so many people can no longer cope with the pressure. It is sad that there are so many young people who see no meaning to life and no reason to go on living.

And your church too, Lord, is experiencing the terror of a stormy night at sea. There have been sad defections. There are clashes of opinion on serious matters which leave people in terrible confusion. There are fewer young people coming forward to commit their lives to the priesthood and religious life.

I notice on the weather charts that at the eye of a storm there is always a low depression. When I get low, Lord, I too feel storms swirling around me. I find myself edgy with anger, very negative and cynical.

And when I am low I easily fall victim to the most vile fantasies and overpowering obsessions. The storms are wild, the night is dark.

I tremble with fear. It is terrifying, Lord. Where have you gone? I remember that you used to be so near to me. Prayer was easy. It was a pleasure. I would feel so convinced of your love. I could sometimes feel it like warmth in my body.

Was it all imaginary? Some form of self-delusion? Don't you any longer care for us, Lord? Or did we have it all wrong when we believed strongly?

Out of the depths I cry to you, O Lord. Lord, hear my voice.

Pause awhile and invite people to get in touch with their own memories of feeling lost and very low in spirit.

A reading from the holy gospel according to Mark (6:45-52)

Immediately, Jesus obliged his disciples to get into the boat and go ahead of him to the other side, towards Bethsaida, while he himself sent the crowd away. And having sent the people off, he went by himself to the hillside to pray.

When evening came, the boat was far out on the lake while he was alone on the land. Jesus saw his disciples straining on the oars, for the wind was against them, and before daybreak he came to them walking on the lake; and he was going to pass them by. When they saw him walking on the lake, they thought it was a ghost and cried out; for they all saw him and were terrified. But at once he called to them, 'Courage! It is me; don't be afraid.' Then Jesus got into the boat with them and the wind died down, so that they were completely astonished. For they had not really grasped the fact of the loaves; their minds were dull.

Are there any words or phrases that particularly strike you in this story? Does the story offer you hope?

Reflecting on the Word

We can apply this story to the boat of the church caught up in the storms of life. The fact that it was dark increased the sense of terror.

Jesus was not with them that night. He had gone up the hills to pray. This represents the time after the Ascension of Jesus. He is no longer physically with us but he is all the time observing us and supporting us in prayer. In heaven Jesus is ever living to make intercession for us.

Even when Jesus came to the help of the apostles he did not physically join them in the boat. His appearance was in a spiritual or ghostly manner. We do not physically see, touch or hear Jesus in our storms, but he is with us nonetheless.

In two great ways he sustains our faith. First of all, in his sacred word he constantly reminds us of God's love. We are constantly told to cast away fear and to have courage.

The second great sustenance we have is the Blessed Eucharist. 'I am the bread of life ... my flesh is real food, my blood is real drink. He who eats my flesh and drinks my blood lives in me and I live in him.' We are told that the storm terrified the disciples because they had not seen what the miracle of the loaves meant. Their minds were closed.

If we love the words of God in the bible and if we really appreciate what the Eucharist means, we will not fear any storm or depression. But if our minds are closed, then the waves of depressing news will fill us with darkness and terror.

Let us pray

O Lord, in the storms of life may we know that you are always with us, caring for us in heaven. Lord, hear us.

May we counteract the depressing news around us by drawing joy and hope from your sacred words in scripture. Lord, hear us.

May we appreciate the Blessed Eucharist as the divine bread of life which supports and sustains us. Lord, hear us.

Encourage people to add their personal reflections and prayers.

Jesus replies

My loved one, I hear you cry from the depths of your despair. You think that I am far away but all the while I am near you. So near that I can hear your faintest whisper, not to mention your despairing cries.

In your darkness you want to see: you reach out for physical evidence: you clutch for any sign. But I am asking you to believe in pure faith: faith that is based on my words.

Remember, dear soul, that I am ever caring and interceding for you. And I have left you two tables to nourish the vitality of your faith.

At the table of my word you will hear again the words of divine revelation, the words which were born under divine inspiration. And there you will see that the phrase most often repeated is 'Do not be afraid. Have courage.' It is there for every single day of the year.

My second table for you is the Blessed Eucharist. The disciples on the lake had quickly forgotten the miracle of the loaves. As I had provided for them on land would I not also care for them on sea?

Do you appreciate the miracle of the eucharistic bread? I have left you my flesh to eat and my blood to drink. So why are you afraid, O soul of little faith.

Open up your closed mind. Open up the doors of your faith. Doubt no longer and fear no more. For I am with you to provide for you and for the wellbeing of my church. The gates of hell shall not prevail against Peter's flock. You have my promise.

Every day of your life take my word and read. Your bible is there to be read, not to be a fancy book gathering dust. Why let your mind be depressed by all the bad news? Take the Good News and read it unto your soul's strength. Receive my light, my solace, my healing and my peace. Let my word be your safe anchor in every storm.

And come to me in the Eucharist. When you are worn out by rowing across the seas of life, come and receive my life to sustain you.

And outside the time for Mass come to visit me in the Blessed Sacrament. Come before me and focus your faith on my presence. There before me find your safe harbour where the storm-tossed boat of your soul will find its peace.

Come to me all you who labour and are heavily burdened and I will give you rest.

Closing blessing or prayer.

Miles from God

Prepare mind and soul by quietness and prayer to the Holy Spirit.

 We come to meet Jesus in the name of all who are finding prayer very difficult because their minds are agitated and their peace of soul deeply upset. Even if the feelings expressed here are not mine at the moment, yet my prayer can be on behalf of others who are feeling miles from God.

Introductory Prayer

O Lord, I drag myself before you to pray ... but I cannot pray. I no longer find any peace in coming to you. In fact, prayer only makes me more agitated than ever. I cannot find rest for my racing mind. When I try to slow down and concentrate I find myself being totally torn apart from within. All I want to do is get up and run. To get busy and active, to be involved in anything that will divert my mind from the pressure.

O Lord, you seem so far away from me these times. I am hungering for a sign of your presence, even a small sign. I know that you said that we should not be looking for signs. But I am weak and that is how I feel at the moment.

If only I could see you for a brief moment! If only I could actually hear you speaking to me! Or reach out to touch you! It is so dark in my faith these days.

Yet I remind myself that there were many who saw you and your great miracles, who heard you preaching, and yet they remained unmoved. They wanted still more signs. In fact some were moved to jealousy and hatred of you. So I must struggle on in faith, without physical signs.

O Lord, how long the night before the sun rises with a new

day? How far the painful journey before we reach the place of rest? How long the struggle before the victory is won?

Sometimes, Lord, I am deeply afraid. Afraid of the sin that lurks within me and I might not be able to hold out against it. Afraid to trust myself totally to you because the price you ask might be too demanding. Afraid that my very faith will collapse and that I will lose all faith in you and in spiritual realities.

And, Lord, there are times when I find it hard to come to you in prayer because I am so disappointed at the way you have let things happen. I get angry when I think of the way people have ignored me and sometimes deliberately hurt me. If this is your will, then I find it hard to accept. It is hard to distinguish whether this is all just my anger or are you angry too.

I can identify with the psalmist who cried out to you:

How long, O Lord, will you be angry with us?
Is your anger to burn like a fire forever?

I feel so far away from you that my faith is now in exile, longing to come home to the experience of your presence. Your love is a word I hear but a reality I do not feel. My soul is a dry weary land without water.

I am thirsting for you, my God, my fountain of living water.
O when can I enter and see the face of God.
Let your face smile once more on your servant, Lord.

Can you relate to this exile of the soul from God's joy? When your faith is dark, do your struggle on in prayer or do you give up trying?

A reading from the holy gospel according to John
(14:26-31)

From now on the Helper, the Holy Spirit whom the Father will send in my name, will teach you all things and remind you of all that I have told you.

Peace be with you; I give you my peace. Not as the world gives peace do I give it to you. Do not be troubled; do not be afraid. You heard me say: 'I am going away, but I am coming to you.' If you loved me, you would be glad that I go to the Father, for the Father is greater than I.

I have told you this now before it takes place, so that when it does happen you may believe, for I will no longer speak to you. Now the ruler of this world is at hand, although there is nothing in me that he can claim.

But see, the world must know that I love the Father and that I do what the Father has taught me to do. Come now, let us go.

Pause to develop your own reflections on these words of Jesus. Are you aware of the Holy Spirit in your life? What is the peace of Jesus as distinct from what the world has to offer?

Reflecting on the Word

This gospel is a great message of peace and consolation for those times when we feel far distant from God or for times of intense temptation. Jesus spoke these words to prepare the disciples for the time when they would no longer enjoy the privilege of his physical presence.

This time after Jesus, in one sense, is a sort of exile since we cannot see Jesus or physically hear his voice. But in another sense, we are not exiles since we have received the Holy Spirit who lives within us. So Jesus consoled the disciples with the promise of a double gift.

The first gift is the Holy Spirit who teaches us through our growing faith. We no longer depend on the physical voice of Jesus since the voice of the Spirit is given to us in the gift of faith.

The second gift is peace of soul. Notice that Jesus spoke of peace on the very night when all hell was about to break loose. But he knew that the devil was powerless against him. He spoke of peace even as he was aware of the suffering which he was soon to face.

Where did his inner peace come from? From his total union in love with the Father's will. How consoling it is to remember that Jesus has left us this inner peace. 'I give you my peace', he said.

His peace is no worldly attempt to escape suffering but the inner strength to cope with any situation. Nor did he remove us from all temptation. But he gave the inner power to resist all the wiles of 'the ruler of this world'. His peace is from the Holy Spirit, deep within the soul, underneath all the storms which disturb the surface of life.

Relaxation techniques or the exercises of yoga can bring great relief from stress. But the peace of Jesus is even greater. It is more than freedom from stress. It is a powerful sense of God's Holy Spirit being with us as our strength and Helper.

Total peace comes only when the Spirit of Jesus raises up our minds and wills unto complete union with the will of the Father. In his will is our peace.

Let us pray

Lord Jesus, you found inner peace in your union with the Father's will: strengthen our love for the Father. Lord, hear us.
Lord Jesus, you did not fear all that Satan plotted against you: make us strong against his darkness. Lord, hear us.
Lord, help us to know how near you are to us through the presence of the Holy Spirit in our souls. Lord, hear us.

Encourage personal observations and prayers.

GATHER IN MY NAME

Jesus replies

My dear friend, my heart goes out to you in your distress. Although you are in darkness, fear not for I can see you. Although you may feel in exile, you are at home for I am with you and in you. Although you are weak and distressed, do not be troubled for I am your strength.

Believe in me. Believe in my presence beyond the reach of your earthly eyes. It is with the heart that you believe, not with the eyes. Many who saw me with their eyes and heard me with their ears did not believe in me with their hearts.

I have not deserted you. In heaven I am ever living to make intercession with the Father for you.

Believe in the Holy Spirit whom you received in your baptism. In the power of the Holy Spirit the work of your inner transformation has begun. You are being raised up from being a creature of earth to being somebody already sharing in heavenly life.

You have been born from above in the power of the Spirit. But you are still a pilgrim on the way and your earthly passions have not ceased to trouble you. You still have to face temptations and spiritual conflicts. But be strong for I have overcome Satan and I am at your side.

As you follow my way to the Father you must bravely share in my dying. Baptism means dying with me as well as rising in the power of the Spirit. Every day you must be determined to die unto sinfulness so that your sharing in the life of the Spirit will be ever more manifest.

Beware of that presumption which would make you think that being born again of the Spirit would make you an instant saint. You still have to wrestle with temptation and struggle with darkness.

As you are tossed about in life seek the depths of your soul where the Spirit rests. If your mind is agitated do not further distress it by a frenzied search for words. Turn in simple quietness to the Spirit within. Invite the Spirit within you to pray in you and through you.

Let the Spirit lead you to the Father's will. Only there, in the

Father's will, can you find the totality of peace and the tranquil sea of perfect order.

Come to me, dear friend, in the Blessed Sacrament of the Eucharist. In the action of the Mass come and be nourished from my own sacrificial banquet. And come in the time after Mass to pray before the tabernacle. Be at home with the Blessed Sacrament of my presence.

Know that I am with you, out of love for you. Lay down your cares. Let my love flow into you to give you peace. Do not let your heart be troubled or afraid.

Close the meeting with a hymn or prayer and blessing.

In times of bitterness

Prepare for prayer in quietness and invocation of the Holy Spirit.

 Once we begin to take prayer seriously we realise that it calls us to great self-honesty. The light of God shines into the hidden corners of heart and mind. We become painfully aware of the residues of bitterness and intolerance which remain in us.

Introductory Prayer

O Lord Jesus, every time I hear of your love and forgiveness I feel deeply ashamed of the amount of unchristian bitterness that remains in my heart.

When I read how you forgave your persecutors, I realise that your love rose above all smallmindedness and revenge. You would not allow the wrongs of others to poison your love. I know what your ideal is but I find I am always struggling in mind, in heart and in tongue.

My mind is so quick to pick up the faults of others.I don't make the sort of allowance for others that I would wish to be made for myself. I pick up one feature, one comment they make, one action done. And this fault obsesses my mind so much that I forget everything else that would balance the picture.

I am ashamed of the smallness of my heart when it comes to tolerance of others and their right to be different. I focus on something small and let it prejudice me against a person. It can be as trivial as their accent, their hairstyle or where they come from. The barriers go up and my doors are slammed shut. Then I am surprised later when I come to know the person more completely.

Because of the negativity in my mind and heart I find it hard to control my tongue. How often have I made the resolution not to harm somebody's reputation only to hear my tongue trip out with the sharp comment or the sniping remark thinly veiled as a joke.

Forgiving others when they have hurt us ... that is surely the most demanding ideal you have put before us. When I feel hurt by somebody's attitude or remark, it is very hard not to let my heart become poisoned.

Trying to forget is impossible because what has happened is imprinted for all time on the mind. What you ask of me, Lord, is to remember with love rather than with bitterness. That is where I so desperately need your help. On my own, by my own natural powers, I cannot reach that sort of remembrance which is totally bathed in the golden light of love.

How did you do it on Calvary? Where did you find that depth of love to pray for those who mocked you, misinterpreted your words, beat you, spat at you? In my weakness, I confess that without your help I will be forever imprisoned in bitterness and negativity.

I hand over my memory to you to transform it into a reservoir where everything is healed by love.
I open my heart to you that it may be healed of its bruises and become a dynamic source of reconciliation.
I give you my tongue that my words may be purified of all sharpness, bitterness and sarcasm.
Lord Jesus, transform me by your love. Heal me at the depths of mind and heart.

Reflect awhile on your own problems in forgiving others or in accepting their different ways. Do the wrongs which others do poison your thoughts with bitterness?

GATHER IN MY NAME

**A reading from the holy gospel according to Luke
(9:51-56)**

As the time drew near when Jesus would be taken up to heaven he made up his mind to go to Jerusalem. He had sent ahead of him some messengers who entered a Samaritan village to prepare lodging for him. But the people would not receive him because he was on his way to Jerusalem. Seeing this, James and John his disciples said, 'Lord, do you want us to call down fire from heaven to reduce them to ashes?' Jesus turned and rebuked them, and they went on to another village.

What is the passage saying to you? Share your ideas with the others. Were James and John tuned into the mind of Jesus?

Reflecting on the Word

Perhaps we can easily identify with the reaction of the two apostles. How would we feel if the door were slammed on our face? How do we react when we meet with bitterness? This story shows how the attitude of Jesus contrasts with the fiery response of some of the apostles.

Any hatred or prejudice is regrettable. Worse again when the hatred is on religious grounds. Jews and Samaritans had a long history of mutual hatred. The prejudice of the Samaritans was at its blackest when Jews were going to Jerusalem for religious purposes.

But two wrongs do not make a right and the apostles, James and John were no better in their reaction. The Jewish ethic allowed an eye for an eye and a tooth for a tooth. Equal vengeance was considered fair game. But Jesus wanted to change all that. Christian love must be bigger than all bitterness: beauty must be beyond the claws of ugliness.

Notice the words of the apostles. They did not ask Jesus to call down fires of revenge from heaven but 'do you want us' to do it! What warped notions they had about the powers that Jesus promised them.

The gospel says that Jesus rebuked them. Rebuking was always the sharp reply of Jesus to the suggestions of the devil. Vengeance, which seeks somebody's comeuppance, is the work of the devil. Justice, which seeks to correct the individual and to restore social order, is the work of God. It is not uncommon to hear people demanding justice when what they are really seeking is vengeance.

The apostles would indeed see fire descend from heaven: not fires of destruction; but the living flame of Pentecost filling them with the Holy Spirit of divine love. It was this Spirit of love who enabled Jesus to forgive his persecutors and to raise the bitterness of Calvary to the level of prayer. He did not come to destroy life but to save.

The tactic of Jesus regarding the inhospitable village is interesting. He simply chose to ignore the hatred and to move on to another village. In other words he avoided a confrontation. It takes prudence to know when confrontation is likely to do more harm than good. There are many instances in life when problems are not solved but are better bypassed or ignored: like avoiding a traffic jam rather than forcing a bullish way through it.

But there are also times when the conflict cannot be avoided. Jesus had to face the full brunt of hatred on Calvary. He did not respond to bitterness with further hatred. Instead, he kept on loving and he prayed for his persecutors.

The episode offers us many challenging questions:
How do I react to the person who has given me a raw deal? *(Pause)*
Why is it that my initial reaction to somebody is always negative? *(Pause)*
Do I seek vengeance or true justice when I have been hurt or wronged? *(Pause)*

Let us pray
Lord, heal the roots of those sore memories which poison
my thoughts and reactions. Lord, hear us.
Strengthen our resolve never to let our love be poisoned by
the wrongs that others do. Lord, hear us.
May the heavenly fires which you send down be fires of
divine love which bring life rather than destruction. Lord,
hear us.

*Allow time for your own observations and
prayers.*

Jesus replies

My dear chosen one, lift up your hearts to heavenly
thoughts and let your earthly bitterness behind. Raise up the
eyes of your heart to long for the heavenly Jerusalem which
is the destiny of your life. Set your feet on a way of life wor-
thy of your calling.

You have already been given a beginning of divine life,
planted as a seed in your soul at baptism. Believe in the life
that you have received. Desire to grow in that life. Every day
implore the Spirit you received to bathe your mind in divine
light and to nurture your heart with the warmth of divine
love. Concentrate on the beauty of your calling and leave all
ugliness behind.

It is inevitable that your life will run up against clashes and
contradictions. Most of these will be unintentional, although
at first you may be inclined to suspect ill-will.

Sometimes, it is true, people do act out of sheer malice. But if
another chooses to be malicious and bitter, why must you
react with a similar poison?

Never let your resolution of love be turned aside by what

others say or do. You have received the waters of divine life at baptism. Do not let these rivers of love be polluted or poisoned by outside happenings.

Frequently meditate on the divine love which has been shared with you. Why do you continue to think and act as if you were not sharing in my life?

You have seen how my beloved disciple, John, thought and acted in his younger days. A veritable son of thunder calling down fires of vengeance. Now consider what he wrote when he had matured in the power of the Spirit: 'This is the love I mean: not our love for God, but God's love for us. Let us love one another since love comes from God.'

Do not let your mind be darkened by an obsession with the hurts you have received. Raise up your heart to the great destiny to which you have been called. Desire the healing of the Spirit in your mind and memory. Let your inner spiritual strength bear fruit in patience, gentleness, kindness and basic goodness towards all.

Come to me in the Eucharist to be strengthened in the life of the Spirit. Remember, dearly beloved one, that unless you eat my flesh and drink my blood, you will not have life in you.

Finish your time of prayer with a hymn or blessing.

Confused and angry

Reach into quietness for a few minutes and implore the help of the Holy Spirit in your prayer.

 There are many situations in life when it can be very hard to discern the loving presence of God. Suffering occurs which leaves people very confused about God's love. Being honest about it, we may be very angry with God. Then, as we meet Jesus, we need to talk to him about our confusion and anger.

Introductory Prayer

O Lord, I come to you very angry tonight. I have met this family whose lives have been shattered by an appalling tragedy. They go to church, say their prayers, obey your law and are good neighbours to all around them. Yet you have let their lives be shattered. You have given them a raw deal.

Why this good family, Lord? Surely they are entitled to ask you, where were you? Where has your protection and blessing been?

It is all a big mystery. There is nothing quite so confusing as the problem of suffering. I have come across people who constantly read your bible and keep talking about the abundant life that you have promised to those who fear you and obey your commandments. They quote the fulness that Job received after his troubles.

But there is another side to that coin, isn't there? If health and prosperity in abundance are a signs of your blessing on the good life, is it equally true that mishap or disaster are signs of punishment for sin? When we see people experiencing failure, family break-up, accidents or financial disaster, are we to conclude that you are punishing them for not living according to your law?

Then again, I meet people who are pushing some particular holy picture or the message of some private visionary. They tell us that if this special picture is hung in the home or some particular prayer is said, you will guarantee safety there. But isn't that very smallminded, Lord, that your protection should stand or fall on the basis of a picture or a prayer.

Your cross, Lord, has always been a great mystery. I am not at all comfortable with the idea that the cross was a punishment demanded by an angry Father for the sins of humanity. I cannot accept the prayer or hymn which speaks of the dreadful wrath of God.

I know that you accepted the cross as a way of showing the extent and depth of your love for us. And your suffering stands for us as an example of how to suffer without bitterness or vengeance.

But there must be further reasons for allowing the cross in your own life and ours. I believe that your reasons are always motivated by love. But sometimes it is very hard to see that love. Lord, help me to see more clearly.

I trust in your love. But sometimes you are so hard to understand. Help me to accept your mystery.

Reflect on your own experience of being disappointed, confused or angry with God. Does God punish people with illness or accidents?

A reading from the holy gospel according to Luke (13:1-9)

One day some persons told Jesus what had occurred in the Temple: Pilate had Galileans killed and their blood mingled with the blood of their sacrifices. Jesus replied, 'Do you think that these Galileans were worse sinners than all the other

Galileans because they suffered this? I tell you: no. But unless you change your ways, you will all perish as they did.

And those eighteen persons in Siloah who were crushed when the tower fell, do you think they were more guilty than all the others in Jerusalem? I tell you: no. But unless you change your ways, you will all perish as they did.'

And Jesus continued with this story, 'A man had a fig tree growing in his vineyard and he came looking for fruit on it, but found none. Then he said to the gardener: 'Look here, for three years now I have been looking for figs on this tree and I have found none. Cut it down, why should it use up the ground? The gardener replied: 'Leave it one more year, so that I may dig around it and add some fertiliser; and perhaps it will bear fruit from now on. But if it doesn't, you can cut it down.'

Did Jesus see tragedies as punishment from God?
Does God want to cut down the fruitless life?

Reflecting on the Word

There are people who constantly feel under threat of punishment from God. When an illness comes or a misfortune strikes, their first thought is that this must be a punishment from God for some wrong they had committed. I must have had it coming to me!

In this gospel episode Jesus tries to break the connection between tragic mishaps and punishment for sin. He takes up two recent tragedies which were fresh in peoples' minds: the shocking incident when Pilate, suspecting a Jewish uprising, invaded the sacred temple area and hacked down the Galileans who were offering sacrifice; and the tragedy at Siloah where eighteen people were crushed when a tower collapsed. Jesus told the people to stop saying that these victims were worse sinners than any others. These tragedies were not the acts of a punishing God.

Most Jews of Jesus' time were mentally stuck with two ideas inherited from the Old Testament. First, they had the ethical idea that justice meant getting the score evened up. Therefore equal revenge was acceptable. A corresponding punishment ought to match every wrong. And this applied to God's affairs as much as to the human domain.

The second inherited idea came from the early period before they had developed a clear belief in life after death. In the absence of an afterlife, then God had to exact his punishment in this life. So, when they saw someone having bad luck they immediately assumed that this was God getting in his stroke of punishment.

Some bible-quoters of today repeat these Old Testament ideas. They are quick to ascribe various addictions or nervous disorders to the punishing hand of God. And they even go back beyond personal sin and say that punishment now may be due to the sins of some previous generation in our family tree. It is amazing how much of the Old Testament and how little of the gospel one finds in these so-called evangelical groups.

What we read in the gospel is that Jesus wants us to stop associating misfortune with punishment for sin. Remember the healing of the blind man when people openly asked whether the blindness was due to the man's own sins or his parents'. Jesus clearly stated that the ailment had nothing to do with anybody's sin. Nor were these two recent tragedies to be linked with punishment for guilt.

In the Sermon on the Mount, Jesus taught that avenging punishment was so far removed from God's mind that he made the sun shine and the rain fall equally for bad people and good.

The justice of God is not about punishment but about correcting the individual and restoring correct order in society. God, who still loves the sinner, desires conversion of ways. Like a gardener who loves each tree, he wants to offer yet one more chance to the fruitless one.

GATHER IN MY NAME

But this may involve digging deep. Digging suggests a painful process. But if we continue to trust in God's love we will experience deep healing in those experiences which initially made us angry with God.

One final point. Jesus warned 'unless you change your ways, you will all perish.' The way of sin is the road to unhappiness. Sin contains its own in-built punishment in the loss of inner peace. And sin's ultimate punishment is in the final rejection of God and his eternal love.

Let us pray

Lord Jesus, as you accepted the cross in loving obedience to the Father's will, help us to accept our crosses in union with you. Lord, hear us.

O loving Lord, move us away from all thoughts of a vindictive, punishing God, towards a greater appreciation of divine love. Lord, hear us.

O Lord, remove our fears about digging for the truth at the roots of our behaviour. Lord, hear us.

Invite people to add their own thoughts and prayers.

Jesus replies

O my dear friend, you are precious in my eyes. Not for one moment do I let you out of my sight. My love for you is constant and unwavering.

There is no situation in life beyond my seeing. And there is no abyss of life that my love has not reached.

Do not imagine that I am absent because on the surface of life things are not going well. Has the sun lost its great furnace of heat just because you do not feel it? Has the moon lost its silver light when you do not see it? Have I ceased to love you when I am correcting you or trying to draw you to a greater depth of life?

My precious one, do not neglect to meditate on my passion and cross. The cross is an open book to teach you about my love. In the book of the cross you will read about suffering and death. You will see the sorrow of my mother. You will see me as the victim of injustice and ill-will.

I know what it is to look for my friends in time of trouble only to search in vain. I trembled and sweated blood in the fear of what I had to face.

It was for love of you that I went into all these experiences of suffering. Whatever form your particular Calvary takes, there you shall meet me and experience my love as never before.

Stay with me in prayer. Do not lose confidence. The eyes of a superficial life cannot see through darkness. Only the eyes of faith will penetrate the dark mysteries of life.

Come to me in the Eucharist where I will strengthen you in the pattern of my death and resurrection. The mystery of your faith is centred on death and resurrection. I desire to lead you ever deeper into this mystery. Stay with me in prayer. And in your darkest moments cling to your faith and keep repeating: Christ is with me, Christ is within me.

Close the meeting with a hymn or blessing prayer.

With all who suffer

Prepare your mind and heart in quietness and prayer to the Holy Spirit.

 In this meeting with Jesus we move beyond ourselves to open up our hearts to the distress of others. In prayer we intercede for all who are heavily burdened with suffering in any form.

Introductory Prayer

We come to pray,Lord, on behalf of those who are struggling with pain of any sort. We pray for those who are weakened by illness or burdened with constant pain: for those with long-term sores or handicap: for all who are facing painful treatment: and for those who are coming to terms with terminal illness.

Pause after each section to mention the names of people either in silence or aloud.

We remember those who are in mental distress and who can find no peace of mind or joy of heart: those who are depressed: who are fretful and anxious about everything: those who suffer from a lack of confidence. (*Pause*)

We intercede for all who are going through emotional distress: those who are lonely after a bereavement: whose trust has been betrayed: who are angry because they have been hurt: or who are suffering after a family break-up. (*Pause*)

We remember all who suffer out of their love and care for others: for children whose lives are damaged by their parents: for parents who worry deeply over their childrens' behaviour. (*Pause*)

We remember with compassion all alcoholics and drug addicts: and those who are hurt by somebody's addiction: for those who have lost all respect for themselves: and for all who carry heavy burdens of guilt from their past. (*Pause*)

We reach out to your light in the name of all who are experiencing spiritual anguish: for those who labour in darkness through a crisis of faith: for those who see no meaning to life and no reason to go on living: for those prayerful souls who are suffering in the wounding of your love. (*Pause*)

We pray for those who are the victims of injustice: for prisoners of conscience: for all who stand up to unjust regimes: and for those who are mocked because of their loyalty to the way of the gospel. (*Pause*)

We pray for those who have no home to sleep in tonight: for those who will toss and turn in search of sleep: and for all who are deprived of sleep by the noises and demands of others. (*Pause*)

A reading from the holy gospel according to Luke (5:12-16)

One day in another town, a leper came to Jesus. Bowing down to the ground, the leper said, 'Lord, if you want to, you can make me clean.'

Stretching out his hand, Jesus touched the man and said, 'Yes, I want to. Be clean.' In an instant the leper was healed. Then Jesus instructed him, 'Tell this to no one. But go and show yourself to the priest. Make an offering for your healing, as Moses prescribed; that should be a proof to the people.'

But the news about Jesus spread all the more, and large crowds came to him to listen and be healed of their sicknesses. As for him, he would often withdraw to solitary places and pray.

 *What are your own thoughts out of this reading? Was there more to the ministry of Jesus than healing the sick?*

Reflecting on the Word

Two points in particular call for deeper reflection: the fact that Jesus touched the leper; and the way that Jesus would leave the crowd and give priority to his time alone with the Father.

It was probably not a case of full blown leprosy since the man was still in the town. However, any form of skin disease was sufficient to bar him from taking part in religious services or public gatherings. Hence, his cure had to be officially certified by the priests. When Jesus touched him, then in the eyes of the law Jesus too was rendered ritually unclean. It shows how much he entered into our condition. He did not stand off at a safe distance. So total was his compassion that the words of Isaiah were fulfilled: 'He took away our infirmities and took on himself our diseases.' (Is. 53:4) Jesus does not stay remote from us in our difficulties but is in very close touch with us.

There were other people in the town sick and in pain. Yet Luke makes the point that Jesus would leave them there to spend time alone with the Father in prayer. The healer must take adequate care of self. Otherwise one will be so drained as to be of no further use to anybody.

Jesus in his human limitation appreciated his need to spend time alone in prayer. It was from his divine union with the Father that his power of healing came.

Although healing the sick was a great ministry, yet Jesus had to leave it to advance his wider ministry in accordance with the Father's will. Sometimes we must leave a good work to have the freedom to meet the demands of a greater call.

Like Jesus we too are called to touch the leper: to do all we can to alleviate the sufferings of others. But sometimes the removal of pain does not happen and God allows people to remain in suffering. Then we must help people to explore the possible blessings that God has in store with the cross. Countless people have testified to the rich blessings they discovered precisely in the sufferings which God permitted to come their way.

Let us pray

O Lord, you were moved in compassion to heal many people: we humbly beg you to work miracles of healing and releasing this night. Lord, hear us.

We pray for your power to work through the skilled hands of surgeons, the tender care of nurses and the wise words of counsellors. Lord, hear us.

Lord, we face the mystery that not everybody is healed. So we pray for those who will continue to carry the cross. Grant them a deep faith so that they might not feel distant from you but very close to you on your cross. Lord, hear us.

Encourage people to add their own thoughts and prayers.

Jesus replies

My dear friend, I am deeply touched by your concern for others. It pleases my heart to see you leave your selfish concerns behind to take on the pain of others and to intercede on their behalf.

It is important that you should pray for others. But make sure that your words are not a cover-up for lack of action. Words are empty if you do not offer practical help that is within your scope. What use is it to tell somebody in trouble that you will pray for them while you refuse to do anything practical?

I want you to appreciate how much I suffered in my passion. My great pity for all who were suffering drew me into sharing in their lot. I could not just say that I loved them while staying at a safe distance.

Meditate regularly on my passion: how I entered into all sorts of pain, physical, emotional and spiritual.

GATHER IN MY NAME

My physical pain was real, you know. The lashes on my back tearing off lumps of flesh: those piercing thorns: the heavy crossbeam falling on me and numbing my muscles further.

My heart cried out in loneliness for a companion to share the journey with me. But I was rejected, betrayed, misunderstood and deserted by my friends.

I entered even into the dark night of spiritual dereliction. I am telling you all this so that you might know that you can meet me in all suffering. However low you descend, I have been in there before you. If you will explore your suffering with faith you will discover my presence there and you will appreciate me as never before.

While on earth, I used to leave the pains of the world and seek out solitude with my Father. You too must climb the mountain of solitary prayer so that you might receive the light of the Father's wisdom.

You must not let yourself be misled by the superficial culture of today into thinking that what matters most are the external trappings of success and physical well-being. I invite you to explore the deeper potential that your Creator-Father has planted in you. There are seeds of true greatness and inner sanctity which come to flower only when you transcend all self-seeking. It is in dying to selfishness that you will find your true life and potential.

The way of the cross is the only way into the fulness of resurrection.

So, when crosses come your way, try to die to self and take up your cross and follow me. In the cross you will find that I am with you.

And my Spirit will bring to flowering the many levels of life which are yours to discover.

Finish your prayer with a suitable hymn or prayer and blessing.

With Mary

Settle in quietness to dispose yourself for prayer.

Many people like to come to Jesus in the company of Mary his mother. They remember that, in the gospel, she exercised an important role in several of the great events of God's grace. Now in heaven she is our mother who leads us straight to Jesus and the divine will.

Introductory Prayer

O Lord Jesus, we thank you for all your gifts. Today we thank you especially for your parting gift ... the gift of your dying words ... the gift of Mary to be the mother of all beloved disciples. Parting gifts are specially planned by the giver and deeply treasured by the receiver.

O Jesus, we deeply appreciate your thoughtfulness and care in leaving us Mary as our mother. You sensed our need of a mother's love to give a very human expression to God's love.

Sometimes we are lost in the infinite distance of God's majesty and we need the understanding of a mother on our journey. Or when we are confused by all the big words and abstract ideas, then we need to focus on the human model that Mary is.

She will always direct our straying paths back to you. At Cana, she told the servants to do whatever you told them. What mother would ever draw people away from her son!

She has the mother's heart which sensed the possible embarrassment of the family at Cana ever before a word was said about the shortage of wine.

Many of us who struggle with religion can at least appreciate the gift of a heavenly mother. We approach her as the backdoor into heaven. We love to call her the refuge of sinners and the consoler of the afflicted.

Lord Jesus, you alone are the one true way to the Father. You alone are our true priest and divine mediator. But in our human weakness we feel stronger in our prayer when we come to you with Mary. For she has access to your heart as only a mother has. As her children we are happy to avail of her intercession.

Lord Jesus, we deeply appreciate the significance of your parting gift, your own mother to be our mother also.

Lord Jesus, we thank you for the gift of Mary.

A reading from the holy gospel according to John (19:25-27)

Near the cross of Jesus stood his mother, his mother's sister Mary, who was the wife of Cleophas, and Mary of Magdala. When Jesus saw the Mother, and the disciple, he said to the Mother, 'Woman, this is your son.' Then he said to the disciple, 'There is your mother.' And from that moment the disciple took her to his own home.

Spend some time pondering on this event. What, do you think, did Jesus mean when he said, 'There is your mother'?

Reflecting on the Word

There are only two episodes in John's gospel where Mary is mentioned: at the wedding in Cana and by the cross on Calvary. Cana and Calvary are connected in the way that in both places Jesus addressed his mother as 'Woman'. To us it sounds cold and impersonal. But in the Aramaic dialect which Jesus spoke, the word for woman sounded very like the name Eve, the first mother. Had Jesus addressed her as 'Mother' he would have been talking to her as his own mother only. But in addressing her as 'Woman' he is referring to her wider motherhood. She is the Second Eve, the mother of all true believers. The one disciple on Calvary represents all the family of the believing Church.

It is very sad that some people disregard the wisdom of the Church's reflection on the place of Mary in the gospel. They say that nowhere in the bible are we told to pray to Mary. But is it likely that Jesus would have told people to pray to her while she was still alive? Not everything is contained in the actual words of the bible. Even a little reflection on the word 'Mother' would reveal her role in helping us from heaven. Hopefully, those who are excited about being 'born again' will progress from infancy into a mature, reflective faith!

Authentic Catholic devotion to Mary has grown out of mature reflection on the gospel. According to the bible Mary played a significant role at all the vital moments of Christ's mission: at his birth, his first miracle and his death. And she was actively present at many of the great moments of the Holy Spirit's coming. She was herself filled with grace under the sacred shadow of the Spirit. It was at her coming that Elizabeth was filled with the Holy Sprit. And the unborn child danced in Elizabeth's womb to the divine music heard in Mary's greeting.

It was Mary who asked Jesus for that first miracle which brought the grace of faith to the disciples. And we notice that she was at prayer with the disciples in the Upper Room before the coming of the Spirit on the newborn Church. She who was the mother of Jesus Christ in his physical body was a prayerful midwife at the birth of his mystical body, the Church.

Mary in no way threatens the unique position of Jesus as the source of all saving grace. St. Paul wrote to Timothy that there is only one mediator between God and man, himself a man, Jesus Christ (1 Tim. 2:5).

However, it was that same mediator, Jesus Christ, who said to the disciple 'There is your mother.' What does a mother mean to her children except the person they go to in their needs, for she watches over them in a very special way?

Not only is Mary the mother who helps us but she is our greatest model in responding to the grace of God. John says that she stood at the foot of the cross. It is a strong picture, indicating a very firm faith at the moment when the sword of sorrow must have been twisting in her heart.

Let us pray
Lord Jesus, we thank you for your parting gift of Mary to us to be our mother. We praise you for her greatness in grace. Lord, hear us.
O Lord, may those who are newly 'born again' grow up in the maturity of faith which accepts Mary as our mother who intercedes for us. Lord, hear us.
May the loving obedience of Mary to the the Father's will be an inspiration to us to do likewise. Lord, hear us.

 *You may wish to share your own favourite ways of devotion to Mary.*

Jesus replies

My dearly beloved disciple, how right you are to look upon Mary as the mother in whom you put your trust and the model whom you follow! Mary has the true heart of a mother, full of deep understanding, intuition and compassion.

She was my first disciple. Naturally, the physical bond between us was very important to me. But more treasured still was her spiritual relationship with me in faith. That is why I drew attention to her as a model of how to hear the word of God and put it into practice.

She was the first pilgrim of faith in the way of life which I taught in my public ministry. Remember how her faith was instrumental at my first miraculous sign, given at the wedding in Cana. My disciples, after seeing that first sign of my glory, learned to believe in me. But Mary had faith ever before the sign. That is why she is emerging at Cana as the mother of all believers.

A mother is a cell of life who is multiplied as she transmits life to another. Mary is the believing mother whose faith is transmitted to all other disciples. Just as the first pilgrim of faith in the Old Testament, Abraham, is called the father of believers, so now must Mary be recognised as the mother of all my beloved disciples. I waited until my dying breath on Calvary to make my final appeal to you all to look on her as your mother.

In your dark and lonely times, when you are filled with fear and anxiety, when you are weighed down by troubles, remember that you have my mother. Make a place for her in the home of your heart.

If you want to know what perfect discipleship means, meditate on Mary's life. She is the headline to copy.

A disciple is open to receive the divine word and heavenly grace. See how Mary was totally open to letting it be done to her according to the heavenly word.

A disciple then is one who cooperates with the graces received. Blessed is Mary who believed and who put the word into practice.

A disciple will carefully observe all my commandments. Meditate on Mary, the family woman, diligently observing all that was laid down in the laws of religion.

She is the selfless woman who let me go out from home on my mission to others.

She is the woman of strong faith who stood beside the cross to accompany me into the dark valley of suffering.

She is the woman of the new age of resurrection who prayed with the disciples in the Upper Room.

She is taken up in my glory as a sure sign of hope to all

Christian pilgrims. And in heaven her mother's heart feels for all the sufferings of her children on earth.

O dear disciple whom I love, take her as the model of your pilgrimage of faith. Imitate her virtues. And trust her as your mother.

Close the meeting with a suitable hymn or prayer.

In praise

Settle in quietness to prepare your mind for prayer. Then pray for the help of the Holy Spirit.

 This evening we come to pray with the praise of God in our hearts and on our lips. We meet with Jesus who is the perfect Word of the glory of the Father.

Introductory Prayer

O, praise the Lord, my soul: my soul, give thanks to the Lord. Never forget all his blessings.

O Lord, my soul is filled with your joy and my heart wants to break into songs of thankfulness and praise.

I have been to the vast and powerful ocean, and before its great power, all burdens were lifted from my mind.

I gazed at the ageless mountains and I came to realise how short-lived are my problems and how brief my passing clouds.

I have looked with wonder on the delicacy of a flower and my life was lifted up to a higher plane of sensitivity.

How have I been so blind every day! How have I missed your handiwork in the world all around me! I allow myself to be swallowed up in the small world of my petty concerns and I fail to see your daily miracles of creation.

Too often my prayers have been all about myself. Forgive me, Lord, for being so wrapped up in my own concerns that I've been insensitive to the beautiful messages you reveal every day.

You are great and glorious from all eternity. You are not depending upon our praise. 'Our praise adds nothing to your greatness but is itself your gift.'

I can look at the world and in my head analyse its scientific complexity but my heart might remain far from you. But when I look at anything great or small, and can sense your presence there, that faith is a gift from you. I humbly beseech you to fill me with your gifts of faith and praise.

Open my eyes that I might see you, the Artist, in all the art of creation.

Open my memory to discern the blessings you have bestowed on me all down the years.

Open my heart to be sensitive to the quiet calls of your love to me each day.

Open up the thirst of my soul to be flooded with your Spirit who will pray in me.

The little moments of spiritual joy that I have savoured make me long for the gift of praise. My soul desires your praise.

That I might every day cry out and sing to the glory of your name.

That I might be filled with praise and thanks!

That I might know you, Lord Jesus, as the perfect Word of praise!

That I might grow in the awareness that you are in me, praising the Father!

That I might lend my body to the Spirit who praises the Father from the innermost heart of my being!

Here take the opportunity to recall your own favourite prayers of praise or moments when you were moved to praise God.

A reading from the holy gospel according to Luke (10:21-2)

At that time Jesus was filled with the joy of the Holy Spirit and said, 'I praise you, Father, Lord of heaven and earth, for you have hidden these things from the wise and learned, and made them known to little children. Yes, Father, such has been your gracious will. I have been given all things by my Father, so that no one knows the Son except the Father, and no one knows the Father except the Son and he to whom the Son chooses to reveal him.'

Recall some time when you experienced something of the joy of the Holy Spirit. Did you ever feel a deep need to sing aloud to God ... or to prostrate yourself in worship?

Reflecting on the Word

This passage reveals alot to us about the prayer of praise. It begins in the gift of the Holy Spirit ... 'filled with the joy of the Holy Spirit.' The gift of the Spirit's joy is received and moves the soul to return to God.

Blessing is a double movement. Firstly it is a movement down from God who gives to us. Then, as we become aware of what God has given, we return to God in thanks and praise.

The prayer of praise, then, is a gift to the soul from God. Can we do anything towards receiving that gift? Yes, indeed. Firstly we must desire the gift and beg God for the experience, just the way children will persist in begging for the choice gift. And we should try to live with a very positive frame of mind, expecting to meet God every day. Perhaps God's blessings have been in our life far more often that we have recognised.

Jesus was delighted with the childlike souls who were open to receive the Father's revelation. Children in their humility are good receivers. But the worldly wise were not as open.

GATHER IN MY NAME

'The rich he has sent empty away.'

Jesus, the Word of the Father, is the perfection of praise. And the good news for us is that, through our baptism, we are caught up in his praise. We are incorporated into Jesus. His Spirit is given to us, waiting to expand our lives into hymns of praise. St. Paul tells us that we are called to live unto the praise of the glory of God.

We are called to praise God. We are destined for the eternity of praise in heaven. Let it begin here on earth.

Let us pray
O God, let us experience the joy of the Holy Spirit which filled the soul of Jesus. Lord, hear us.
O God of the child, you reveal the things of heaven and earth to humble souls: open up our minds and hearts to the wonders all around us. Lord, hear us.
O Father, may we know you through all that your Son reveals and teaches. Lord, hear us.

Invite people to add their reflections and prayers.

Jesus replies

Dear child of my love, my heart delights in calling you to raise up your soul in praise of the Father.

In your baptism I took you to myself and planted in you the beginnings of my own divine life. My life is totally unto the glory of the Father. I am the Father's Word of praise. I am the reflection of his glory, the mirror-image of his majesty.

When I adopted you at baptism, I called you into this life of divine praise. My Spirit is given to you to pray within you. You must freely cooperate with the grace of baptism for its seeds to grow.

Let your heart constantly desire the experience of God. Let there be room in your mind to receive divine favours. Be as humble as the child who recognises that he has needs but who boldly expects them to be satisfied. The pride that accompanies self-sufficiency is the greatest obstacle to receiving my gift of praise. When your hands are already full I cannot pour my gifts into them.

Open up your mind to discern my presence in your experiences. Prefer good spiritual reading to empty diversion or time-wasting television. Give yourself time every day to savour the Father's majesty which adorns the created world you live in.

Learn the language of praise from the sacred psalms. And be sensitive to the beautiful fruits of the Spirit which are to be seen in the good people you meet with every day.

Constantly search for what is good and beautiful. Let the ugliness of scandals and sensation pass you by. Invite the Holy Spirit you have received to take over your mind and heart. Let the Spirit pray through you to the rhythm of your breathing. In that way, your breath will be one in harmony with the Breath of God.

Above all, try to appreciate the supreme sacrifice of praise which I have left to you in the celebration of the Blessed Eucharist. The Eucharist goes beyond words into the living movement of divine praise. The celebration of the Eucharist is my return to the glory of the Father in the power of the Holy Spirit.

The Eucharist draws you up into the living memory of my death and resurrection. Now that I am lifted up from the earth, I draw you up to myself. So, at Eucharist, lift up your heart to give praise and thanks to the Father. It is through me, with me and in me, in the unity of the Holy Spirit that all honour and glory is rendered to the Father. Let your life be a great Amen to my praise of the Father.

My dear child in faith, I am the Word of the Father: and I call you to lift up your voice in thanksgiving and praise every day of your life.

Conclude with a hymn or blessing.

GATHER IN MY NAME